# EXPLORING NEW EUROPE
## *A Bicycle Journey*

**Barry D. Wood**

Exploring New Europe: *A Bicycle Journey*
by Barry D. Wood

Copyright ©2017 Barry D. Wood, (econbarry.com)

ISBN: 978-0-9976959-0-8 (Print)
ISBN: 978-0-9976959-1-5 (E-book)

Typography, book and cover design, prepress services:
Kathleen R. Weisel, Bellingham, WA (weiselcreative.com)

Photos by the author, except where noted in captions.

Cover photo: Alexander Nevsky Cathedral, Sofia, Bulgaria.

Back cover photo: The Stone Bridge over the Vardar River, Skopje, Macedonia.

## *Acknowledgements*

Without invaluable assistance from Peter Wilhelm in Cape Town, Ian McDonald in Washington, DC, and the late John Martell in Kalamazoo, this book would not have been written. It is dedicated to my grandfather Fred D. Hilbert and my uncle Robert E. Wood, both of whom encouraged me to travel and learn from it.

# CONTENTS

# INTRODUCTION

This book is an attempt to combine the adventure of cycling 2,500 miles through relatively unknown territory with an introduction into the lives of ordinary people I met along the way. You the reader can decide if I've succeeded.

Barry D. Wood

After the Berlin Wall came down in 1989, I became deeply involved in reporting on the transition to market economies in Eastern Europe. In 1990 I spent a week in what was still the German Democratic Republic and a year later made my first reporting trips to Poland, Czechoslovakia, Hungary and Romania. Two years later I spent ten days in the Baltic States and in 1994 I became the Voice of America correspondent in Prague with the task of reporting on the region's economic transformation. During that three-year assignment I traveled extensively in what had been communist Eastern Europe.

Like most journalists I reported mostly on the words and deeds of government officials and business leaders. In addition I did a considerable number of human interest stories. Nonetheless I came to believe that more emphasis was needed on how ordinary people were coping with profound change.

Consider for a moment what life under communism was. For two generations the state controlled pretty much everything. In most countries private property didn't exist. There was little choice in where you lived or worked. Travel was restricted. Consumer goods were shoddy and in short supply. Prices, rents and wages seldom changed but bore no relation to market forces. Leaders were imposed not chosen. The media was a mouthpiece of the party and government. Individual initiative was discouraged and punished. Fear was pervasive.

After 1989 and the collapse of communism everything changed. Freedom was triumphant. There were free elections, industries were freed from state control, individual liberties expanded. Democratic governments broke with Moscow and sought integration with the west. Reforms were popular but often painful. Living standards remained low and older people in particular were bewildered and struggled to adapt.

The more I traveled in Eastern Europe the more I became aware that the region's diversity in language, culture and traditions were little known by outsiders and even by those in neighboring countries. Upon reflection this isn't surprising as during the communist period not only was it difficult for easterners to get out, it was hard for westerners to get in. Even today with borders open few westerners, for example, know much about Romania, Bulgaria or Albania. I wondered if I could weave this rich tapestry together.

In the autumn of 1995 I hit upon the idea that led to this book. I had arrived by bus in Klaipeda, Lithuania from Kaliningrad, Russia. The regional bus took five hours to traverse the Curonian Spit, the picturesque offshore sand dune shared by Russia and Lithuania that was a closed zone under communism.

An ordinary bus ride became a revelation. In the back a man reeking of vodka annoyed passengers with his drunken singing. In the middle of a forest an elderly couple in rubber boots and carrying pails stood on the roadside signaling the bus to stop. They got on, stood in the aisle, and then soon got off. They waved and vanished into the woods in search of mushrooms.

My seatmate with whom I spoke at length was a schoolteacher returning home after visiting relatives. When we reached the border Lithuanian police came through the bus inspecting passports. Then the Russians, but not the Lithuanians or the lone American, were ordered off for closer inspection. From the window I watched a disagreeable scene of petty humiliation.

Arriving in rainy Klaipeda I made my way to a pizza restaurant and while sitting alone realized that the bus journey was a gift. It had opened a window into the lives of people unknown to most westerners.

I concluded that my contribution would be traveling by land across the entire region and telling the stories of ordinary people. Not wanting to figuratively parachute from one capital city to the next, I wished to go deeper than contacts in airports, taxis and hotels frequented by technical tourists. I would travel by bus or train.

Two years later in 1997 my then 13-year-old daughter and I were traveling by train from the Czech Republic to Romania to visit Dracula's castle at Brasov. Somewhere on the plains of eastern Hungary our train jerked to a halt. Pulling down the window we watched a thin shirtless man in the distance slowly swinging a scythe from side to side mowing a field of hay. After some time he paused, stood the wooden tool on end, removed a whetstone from his pocket and sharpened the blade. His ancestors, I thought, would have done exactly the same thing. Watching this, I wondered who the man was. Did he own the land on which he toiled? How did he feel about the future? At that moment the train jolted forward and the man in the field was gone forever.

It was then that I realized I should make my journey by bicycle. If I had been on a bike, I thought, I could have stopped, waved, walked across the field and engaged the man in conversation. That couldn't happen if I were on a train or bus.

Later our train reached the gentle hills of Transylvania. We observed how haystacks were arranged around a center pole and rudimentary ladders typically leaned against the thatched roofs of cottages. Once I gazed through a window to where a table had been set. If I were on a bike I could knock on the door and might be invited inside.

Having settled on the idea of crossing Eastern Europe by bicycle there were new issues to contemplate. I was already 54; was I physically able to ride through rugged terrain and across formidable mountains? What would be the route? Would it be safe?

I knew little about bicycle touring but luckily I knew someone who did. In October 2000 I persuaded my German friend Peter Schultze to take me along on a six-day ride through Alsace and the Black Forest. It was a wonderful experience, convincing me that my cycling plan was feasible.

Peter, five years older than I, had long been an adventure cyclist. Virtually everything I learned about cross-country cycling came from him. I learned it is critical to pack only what is needed as weight is a major constraint. Peter rode with the panniers or saddlebags in front where it's easier to keep an eye on them. I would do the same. He sought out small guesthouses not just to cut costs but because it was the best way to connect with locals. I did the same. Then there were Peter's maxims for bicycle touring: **be flexible, stay away from main roads, avoid city traffic, and put people and enjoyment ahead of covering territory.**

From that test ride I also learned something I hadn't anticipated. I resolved to do the journey alone. Yes, there is safety in numbers and having a companion can be enjoyable. But I discovered that excessive talk can dissipate the thoughts and impressions you wish to reflect upon and then put in writing at the end of the day. Also, I didn't want to be responsible for another person. I wanted the focus to remain solely on the journey. So despite the risk, I concluded I would ride alone.

In planning the journey, I calculated that I would average 35 to 40 miles a day, just as Peter and I did in the Rhine country. The goal would be discovering new places and people. Studying maps I selected the broad outline of a route that would take me through the greatest number of countries while still proceeding from north to south, from the top to the bottom of Eastern Europe. Choices had to be made. I omitted Ukraine and Belarus. I opted to cross Poland diagonally to connect with eastern Germany and North Bohemia while avoiding the Tatra Mountains on Poland's southern border. Likewise I couldn't touch all of the countries that emerged from the old Yugoslavia. Since I wanted to include Romania and Bulgaria, I would go through only the parts farthest east, Serbia and Macedonia. I omitted Croatia, Slovenia and Bosnia-Herzegovina.

Luckily I had been in all the countries along the route, so I wasn't venturing completely into the unknown. As to communication, I'm not a skilled linguist but I can converse in German and French and rudimentary Czech. I was aware that young people everywhere in the region were learning English.

I calculated that a journey of over 2,000 miles would require at least six weeks. Not once did I contemplate doing the trip in a single go. I didn't have that much vacation and didn't want to be away from home for that length of time. Instead I would divide the journey into segments of 300 or so miles. I would ride my own Cannondale hybrid and bring it with me as accompanied baggage on flights to and from Washington.

By the spring of 2001 I was ready. I would start in Estonia in the far north where I had friends. Before finishing in late 2005 there would be seven trips, each one starting from where I had left off. After finishing the ride I stayed in touch with several people I had met. Regularly from 2007 to 2015 I made return visits. Updates on people are in the epilogue.

Now, what about the title *New Europe*? It's a term that has been used in different contexts for decades. In our time it was coined in 2003 by then U.S. defense secretary Donald Rumsfeld. In January of that year he was annoyed that the French and Germans were not supporting the U.S.-led war in Iraq. So he began using the term New Europe to identify formerly communist countries in the east—Poland and the Baltic States—that endorsed American policy. The label caught on and was used increasingly by the former east bloc nations themselves, most of which joined NATO and the European Union by 2004.

There is also a geographic reason proscribing the use of Eastern Europe as a label for the post-communist nations. The Czechs, for example, are correct to emphasize that Prague lies to the west of Vienna and that Austria is never called Eastern European. Other countries object because to them Eastern Europe means poor. Linguistic controversy extends also to the Balkans where some countries prefer Southeastern Europe as they think Balkans implies lawlessness, violence and poverty.

In writing this book I've been guided by two precepts. One from Mark Twain is, "write what you know." The other came from legendary baseball announcer Ernie Harwell, with whom I became friends in his later years. I asked Ernie how he decided what to include in his weekly columns for the *Detroit Free Press*:

> *What would someone be interested in that I could write, drawing on my own experience that someone else couldn't write because they didn't have that particular experience. And then I go from there.*

What follows is a personal narrative, the story of Barry and his bike and a 2,500-mile odyssey across the plains, woodlands and mountains of New Europe.

# I.

# ESTONIA AND LATVIA

Heikki Saller was my connection to Estonia. Heikki was born in 1966 and we had met several years before my bike trip when he was among a group of young East Europeans who came to the U.S. to learn western techniques of journalism. At that time he was a business reporter for a Tallinn newspaper.

More so than other participants, Heikki was very optimistic. When the group introduced themselves, he held high a two-crown banknote and said the new Estonian currency that had replaced the Soviet ruble tangibly represented Estonia's independence and bright future. His own subsequent progress mirrored that of his country.

When Heikki met my plane in Tallinn he was driving a relatively new German sedan. He had left journalism and started his own public relations firm. He and his wife Meret had two children, had purchased a four-room apartment in the suburbs, and were now borrowing from a bank to renovate their kitchen.

On the evening before I set out Heikki took me to Paldiski, a small town on the Baltic Sea that used to house a Soviet submarine training facility. As we strolled along the beach, Heikki stopped, leaned forward, and with his finger carved parallel lines in the sand.

"During Russian times," he said, "it was forbidden to walk on the beach at night. Each day they used special machines to make stripes in the sand so border guards could tell if anybody had escaped or come ashore."

Listening to my friend's story, the term "Russian times" struck me as odd—as if five decades of Soviet occupation ended not in 1991 but much earlier. There was something else. Heikki said Estonians referred to his generation as "winners" because unlike older people, "if you were 35 or younger when communism ended you had a much easier time adapting to the new world of personal responsibility and free markets."

Heikki Saller on the beach at Paldiski

It was a cool, breezy July 4—the peak of the northern European summer—when I departed from the tidy Estonian capital and headed for Albania, 14 countries and 2,500 miles away.

I steered gingerly into city traffic, pedaling slowly to get used to the weight of saddlebags on the front rack that made turning cumbersome. A steady stream of cars, trolley buses and trucks rolled past, some of them coming uncomfortably close. I was glad that I had mounted an orange safety flag on a short pole above the rear rack. After ten minutes the traffic thinned and I became part of the flow of vehicles headed south towards the Latvian border.

Estonia seems always to be described as tiny. That's wrong: the country is small but it is not tiny. It is as large as Switzerland, or New Hampshire and Vermont combined. What is tiny is Estonia's population, one-and-a-half-million inhabitants.

I left Tallinn with mixed feelings. The city is a lovely mix of modern and medieval with an overlay of communism. Tallinn is more town than city, its 500,000 inhabitants accounting for a third of Estonia's population.

My route through the Baltic states

For centuries the three Baltic States were provinces of Russia. Until the collapse of the Soviet Union they had been independent only for the 20-year period between the first and second world wars.

I was starting from an Estonia that was utterly transformed. Beneath the 14th century gates and turrets peering across Tallinn's Toompea Hill, the Estonian capital glistened with newly built stainless steel and glass hotels that accommodated the surging throng of tourists disgorged daily by ferries and planes from nearby Finland and Sweden.

In what can only be described as an economic miracle, Tallinn has been transformed into a modern, prosperous European city. The grayness and neglect of five decades of communism is gone. Tallinn sparkles like Snow White awakened from slumber.

I rode with increasing confidence until a Y junction without signage posed a dilemma. An equal number of cars headed in two directions. I steered left because that road paralleled the rail line and it seemed logical that Estonia's only railroad would be adjacent to the highway. It didn't take long to realize I was wrong as the road petered out while the rail line veered off. Fortunately it was easy to divert back to the main road.

Soon I was in the country amid fields of sweet-smelling hay and stands of birch and pine, which I would learn cover most of Estonia. I was traveling on the "Via Baltica," the highway that connects the capitals of Estonia, Latvia and Lithuania.

I was riding a Cannondale hybrid, "hand made in the USA" as their slogan used to proclaim. There were twin panniers mounted on the front rack stretched fat and tight with clothes and equipment, each of the rucksacks weighing about 25 pounds. The handlebar bag, always visible with a mere downward glance, displayed beneath its vinyl cover a folded map, and then within writing paper, passport, cell phone, and snacks—currently two apples and a container of drinkable yogurt. At the rear was another rack to which was strapped a duffle bag with other personal effects. I was the rider, a 57-year-old relatively fit, inquisitive American journalist in field shorts, cycling shoes, tee shirt and yellow helmet who was off to meet ordinary people in the several lands that had until recently been communist-ruled.

From the seat of a touring bicycle time moves slowly. In good weather like today minutes and hours slide lazily by in rhythm with the sound of tires rolling on the surface. I focused on the sweet smell of pine boughs and fresh mown hay. Every 90 minutes or so I took a break, usually pulling off the road into a grove of trees and leaning the bike against a tree while I sat down and enjoyed a snack and a few swigs of water.

At 8 PM the sun was still up in the western sky but after six hours in the saddle I was tired and wondering where I would spend the night. The cyclometer said I had traveled 42 miles.

Ahead was the spire of a village church that had become steadily larger as I drew closer. My map told me that I was in the middle of Estonia. The church was in the village of Marjamaa half way between Tallinn and the southern coast. Hoping to find shelter, I diverted from the highway and ventured into the unknown.

I had no illusions about finding a hotel as I had been informed several miles back that there were no hotels this side of Parnu, which was well beyond my reach. What I hoped to find was a safe public place where I could get a few hours' sleep.

Aside from the church there wasn't much to Marjamaa. Twice I rode the short length of its only major street. I found a storefront that appeared to be a bus station but its door was locked. So too was the church door. Aside from a few parked cars the main street was empty and still.

On my second pass I heard voices coming from a basement. Approaching there was the sound of cutlery on dishes. It was the village restaurant.

Parking the bike I paced back and forth and rehearsed some lines that I hoped might get a response. Then, helmet in hand, I went down the steps and walked to the middle of the dimly lit room where perhaps a half-dozen diners were seated at small tables. Slowly but firmly I said, "Will anyone here take in a boarder for the night? I'm a traveler from America and I've come from Tallinn on a bicycle and there is nowhere to sleep."

After a few agonizing seconds, a tall man in the back, 40ish, in short sleeves, put down his fork, raised an arm and said in clear English, "you can stay with me." I was flabbergasted and of course delighted. When he finished and paid the waitress, he beckoned me to follow him outside and then motioned for me to follow his red Opel sedan. I did and soon we arrived at a cluster of two-story stucco buildings adjacent to a field.

Rein Reinok, my benefactor in Marjamaa

Climbing out of his car, my host introduced himself as Rein Reinok, a 41-year-old entrepreneur who owned this duplex where he, his wife and their two boys resided. The family, he told me, was away at the beach. His business was fabricating solar panels for export to Finland, a collaboration that required him to speak English almost daily.

Within minutes of escorting me inside and showing me his internet equipped PC, Rein was on his way to Parnu, the seaside resort some 30 miles away that was my destination for the next day. Before departing, Rein invited me to help myself to food and drink and use the computer to check email. He said he would return in the morning.

Astonished at my good fortune in meeting a person of such trust and generosity, my legs ached as I leaned over the couch to arrange the cotton sheet and pillow that Rein had brought out. Gazing out through the undraped window, the round disk of a setting sun was still visible in the western sky. Sunlight streamed in. It was 10 PM. Exhausted from eight hours and 40 odd miles of riding, I slid beneath the sheet and was asleep within seconds.

I awoke in the morning to see Rein moving about the kitchen. He laid out fruit, bread, cheese and coffee. We talked as we enjoyed this fine breakfast. Then we went outside to see his vegetable garden. Bending over and pulling weeds, he said, "we Estonians aren't happy unless we get our hands into the dirt each summer."

We drove into town and saw his small factory. He took from a drawer blueprints for a planned expansion. In the cramped one-story building, three women sat at a table piecing together small silicon panels connected by plastic rods, tiny circuits that they then held in their hands. Rein was confident that he could expand his business to supply Swedish manufacturers as well.

Rein was clearly a man in a hurry. Like other Estonians I had met, he said the present was the best time ever for his country. He said that when independence arrived in 1991, he knew he must move swiftly. Unafraid to borrow to buy the house he was living in, he borrowed more to start his business. Thirty minutes later we returned to his house. After loading the bike, I thanked Rein and rode off.

As I steered back onto the highway I thought of how both Rein and my friend Heikki back in Tallinn spoke of family members deported by the Russians during and after the Second World War. Heikki said his grandfather, a medical doctor, was exiled to Siberia, because he had treated wounded German soldiers. Rein said his father was sent away because Soviet commissars discovered a copy of Hitler's *Mein Kampf* among his books.

It was another fresh day without clouds or wind. It was well after 10 AM when I left Marjamaa. That wouldn't be a problem, I thought, as my destination was only 30 miles away.

I took my first break at a country store some miles north of Parnu. I was seated on the ground next to my bike. Above me, I heard a voice say in deliberate, clear English: "Where are you going?"

Looking up, I saw an older man wearing a yellow cap,

holding a battered red bicycle, a striped grocery bag over his shoulder. I answered that I had come from Tallinn and hoped to eventually reach Albania at the other end of Europe.

Enno Kuusmets at his house

Enno Kuusmets, I learned, was a 65-year-old pensioner who had taught himself English watching subtitled television programs at his nearby cottage in the woods. "I had nothing else to do," he said. Delighted at this chance encounter, I asked if I could see his home. He said, "of course." Mounting our bikes we rode along a sandy road that went into the woods. Finally there was a path that led through shoulder-high weeds. Enno's cottage then came into view. It was a sturdy one-story affair. Firewood was stacked near the unlocked front door. Overgrown bushes and vines climbed towards the roof.

Enno said he been retired for ten years and subsisted on a government pension of about $80 a month, enough for food and electricity but little else. He confided that his life went off track in 1991 when his wife died and his savings were wiped out in the Estonian hyperinflation that accompanied the breakup of the USSR. "It was," he told me, "a turning point. I lost my money and I lost my wife."

He invited me in. The cottage seemed cozy and comfortable. Newspapers were spread about, and reading glasses rested on the table next to the television's remote control. Enno said he had taught himself English, studying from a book, but mostly from watching English language movies on TV.

Despite difficult circumstances, Enno was relaxed and optimistic about Estonia's future. Independence was a great thing, he told me, and no one wished to return to the past.

Thanking Enno for his time, I pushed the bike back through the tall grass to the road. Riding slowly towards the main road I became absorbed in the beauty and serenity of the place. The only sound was the soft grating of bicycle tires against sand.

Bustling Tallinn seemed a world away, yet I calculated that by car it was probably no more than a two-hour drive. Enno had no car and hadn't been in the capital for eight years. His grown son whom he seldom saw lived far away.

When I arrived in Parnu late in the afternoon, I had traveled 76 miles from the capital. A popular resort in both Czarist and communist times, Parnu was a typical beach town. It was immediately apparent that today most summertime visitors came from Finland and Sweden.

I found accommodation just a few blocks from the sea where an enterprising hotelier had placed prefabricated A-frames at the back of the property for budget travelers. Inside my tiny cabin was the scent of fresh-cut lumber. The bed took up most of the space. As I collapsed onto the bed the sound of a jazz orchestra playing at a festival not far away wafted through the open window.

That evening the streets were crowded with vacationers. Families were out for a stroll after a lazy day in the sun.

Seduced by the serenity I found in Parnu, I didn't get underway the next day until 1 PM.

Despite warnings that between Parnu and the Latvian border there was no accommodation, I rode on hoping I could travel the 36 miles and cross the border by nightfall. As time went by I realized not only that the warnings were correct but that I was unlikely to reach the border that day. At a lonely market I asked the clerk about accommodation. She shrugged and said there was nothing.

About 8 PM a sign on a tree advertised beachfront campsites. I diverted onto a sandy trail and rode the short distance through tall pines to the Baltic shore. At the edge of the parking lot was a hut where a clerk, an older woman, was knitting. Behind her were battered sleeping bags that could be rented for one dollar. I gazed at the ramshackle tents along the shore and resolved to go on. Trying to make myself understood, I asked if there were other places.

At last she produced an ancient rotary telephone. Reading from some penciled lines in a small notebook, she slowly dialed a number. After a perfunctory greeting she passed the phone to me. "Allo," came the booming voice at the other end. I asked if I could speak English—and back came a husky and reassuring, "Yes, of course." The gruff man said he had space in his bed and breakfast about five miles from where I was. He gave clear directions. I thanked the kind lady, mounted up and rode off towards Peep's B&B.

Thirty minutes later at 10:50 PM with darkness falling, I arrived, once again delighted with my good fortune.

Peep, the man with whom I had spoken, stood at the end of the driveway holding a bottle of Saku beer. Tall with white whiskers and a serious demeanor, he seemed happy to greet an American visitor. He carried one of my panniers as we crossed the lawn to a second building where there was a tidy room with single bed, chair, small mirror, and two towels. Peep then asked if I had eaten and quickly invited me to join the small group who were seated around a campfire enjoying a cookout.

Thus was I introduced to shaslyk, Russian-style barbecue from the Caucases. Shaslyk is marinated meat and vegetables on skewers cooked on an open fire, the skewers laid between bricks low and close to glowing embers. There was salad and beer to go with it. Only Peep spoke English but that made no difference. The five others who were speaking Russian or Estonian seemed pleased to have one more person around the fire.

Peep's B&B

The next morning, after a wonderful sleep, I joined Peep beneath an umbrella in the garden. His wife Anne, for whom the B&B is named, brought out cold cuts, fruit, bread and coffee, Peep complained that the summer season was too short for the guest house to be profitable. "There is only June and July," he said, "we don't make any money." (My room cost the equivalent of $20.)

Peep Laul at his B&B near the Estonia/Latvia border

Aware that his property was adjacent to the main road linking two Baltic capitals, I asked if he had considered taking out a bank loan to put up a gasoline station or motel. Surely, I said, he could make a profitable business from the increasing volume of traffic coming across the border three miles to the south. Waving his arm, Peep dismissed my suggestion. "This would mean," he said, "that I would have to start from zero. I'm too old."

Peep said he was 52 but he looked much older. In Soviet times, he continued, he had been a policeman and then a computer programmer. They lived in Tallinn and Anne worked for the city's fire department. Peep said that he was diabetic and had been allowed to retire early with a half-pension. He said he purchased the house and land surrounding the B&B in 1979 for 100 Soviet rubles (roughly $100). It was the family's weekend retreat until 1991 when he and Anne converted it to a B&B.

We talked about life under communism and at some point Peep grew animated and said there was something he would like to show me. Dashing into the house he returned with a hardcover ledger from the 1960s in which he had listed every Beatles recording he heard on the radio. He explained in detail that each entry had a notation of the date individual songs and albums were released in various countries. There was a column for the date Peep first heard each song. During communism, he said with passion, "The Beatles were everything." For those trapped in the Soviet Union, "they represented freedom, the West, and hope."

There was something else about Peep. He loathed Russia. More than once he said, "America must never trust Russia." The bear is still on the prowl, he said, "and would like to again take over little Estonia." I found his critique puzzling since his house guests were Russian-speaking Estonians. His Russian friend Alexander was this morning nursing a hangover, pacing across the yard drinking another Saku beer. Bare-chested with shorts, he paraded at a considerable distance from where Peep and I were seated. Alexander, with a shock of uncombed black hair, called out repeatedly his few words of English, which were, "fine, thank you."

As I loaded the bike, Peep came over to comment about the weather. "Remember," he said only half joking, "that when the wind comes from the east, from Russia, it's always a sign that the weather will be bad." Then in his gruff voice he warned me about Latvia. "Be on guard with Latvians," he said, "they are poorer than we are and suffer from having more Russians among them. You will see."

I felt privileged to learn so much about Peep. He was so different from Rein back in Marjamaa, for while their surnames revealed that they were both ethnic Estonians, I'm sure that Rein would have moved ahead if he owned the B&B. He would have gotten the needed permits and bank loans for a development. Peep, by contrast, was just holding on. He didn't have self-confidence or vision. He was a heavy smoker with health problems already and clearly aware that his best years were behind him. Peep spoke of what he couldn't do. Similarly, age must be a factor. Rein was nearly 20 years younger and looked to the future. Peep bore the scars of hard times and advancing years.

As I rode away and approached the Latvian border, I thought of how lucky I had been these first three days. I had been welcomed into people's homes and had peak experiences that I suspect will forever make me feel fondly towards Estonia.

In three days of excellent weather I had traveled 112 miles and crossed the breadth of Estonia from north to south.

When I set out from Peep's B&B I never contemplated riding all the way to Riga in a single day. It was after all an 80-mile journey, roughly twice the distance I covered on each of my previous days of riding. Even when planning the trip, I thought 55 miles would be a respectable achievement. But the weather was cool and the riding easy.

At 11 AM I arrived at the border with Latvia. It was modern

and efficient with a parking lot, multiple lanes for passing vehicles, a customs office and passport control. Then there was the usual no-man's land and after a few yards a similar collection of buildings on the Latvian side. During Soviet times there was no border, merely a road marker indicating that a traveler had crossed from one Soviet republic to another.

Once inside Latvia it didn't take long to learn that Peep was right. Latvians were visibly poorer. Their appearance suggested harder lives. There was little activity and the infrastructure was less developed.

As the hours went by for the first time I became bored. There were long stretches of empty spaces, untended fields and birch forests. Time slowed down as I pedaled steadily ahead, seldom passing a village. The tedium was broken only when the highway adjoined the sea and I could watch and hear the gentle lapping of waves onto the shore. When I was away from the sea I played mental games trying to discern the smell of salt air, guessing when the sea would again come into view.

I stopped in a village where a solitary fishing boat was tethered to a dock. Among the few woeful buildings, one was larger and appeared to be a fish canning plant that probably accounted for the few jobs that were available. A street carnival was underway but only a handful of people were there. In the one open shop I was unable to get my break time supplies. I hurried on.

Additional hours went by. As before, I had no plan as to where or how I would spend the night. Having twice faced similar challenges that ended with good results, I was not overly concerned as daylight faded and fatigue began to take hold.

Sometime after 6 PM I passed an open but uninviting roadside lodge. Gazing across at the isolated hotel with no cars in the parking lot, I rode on hoping that I could do better. There was still adequate light and despite seven hours of riding, I pressed on. Another hour went by and I came to another hotel nearly identical to the first, but with a view of the sea. It too looked spartan and communist and there were no cars in the lot. Breakfast, I imagined—thinking back to Eastern Europe in the early 1990s—would be a buffet of cold cuts, cucumbers and tomatoes, sliced cheese, and weak tea and coffee. I would be the only guest. I didn't stop.

At 9 PM as dusk blended with near darkness beneath tall trees, I passed a blue and white road sign that read "Riga 30 km" or 18 miles. Doing the math, I calculated that I had already come 60 miles. Couldn't I do another 18? For the first time I seriously thought I might reach Riga that evening.

If there were no hills I could be in Riga within two hours. But how would I make my way through the biggest city in the Baltics in the dark of night?

At 10 PM I switched on the taillight and then the headlight as the roadway was darkened by a canopy of trees. Thirty minutes later I was in the Riga suburbs. Signs no longer said Riga, they simply said the Latvian equivalent of downtown.

At 11 PM I was pedaling along the shoulder of Riga's only freeway. Soon I was on Brivibas (Freedom) Boulevard, which is lined with 19th century apartment buildings like you find in Prague or Vienna. By now I had the bit in my teeth, thrilled at what I had achieved and determined to get to the finish line. I could now see the spires of Riga's many churches as well as the brooding tower of the tall Protestant cathedral in the old town. Reaching the wide Daugava River that bisects the city, I parked the bike and celebrated with a photo of the setting sun.

Crossing the bridge, I pedaled the final half-mile to the SAS Radisson, hoping that the hotel where I had twice stayed would have a room. Locking the bike, I took a pannier in each hand and went inside. I must have been a sorry sight, disheveled and hobbled from fatigue. At the front desk I realized that I was unable to stand up straight.

Luckily there was room and a double bed never looked

better. With a final glance at the nighttime panorama of the old town across the river, I pulled the drapes and collapsed for an extraordinary night's sleep.

In 12 hours I had come 84 miles (128 km) from Estonia.

Sleep is wonderfully restorative. Refreshed and eager to explore fascinating Riga I took the next day off. Riga's population of one million makes it the biggest city in the Baltics. Successively German, Russian, and Latvian, Riga remains an essentially Russian-speaking city, a sore point for ethnic Latvians justifiably bitter at the influx of Russians who arrived after Hitler's defeat.

For 800 years Riga has been a trading center and it remains so today. A northern outpost of the German Hanseatic League, Riga was a principal seaport for Russia. In the embassy district are elegant art deco buildings from the early 20th century. Here lived philosopher Isaiah Berlin and Russian filmmaker Sergei Eisenstein, whose father was a prominent architect. Dancer Mikhail Baryshnikov grew up in Riga.

Russians have lived in Riga as long as Latvians and from previous visits I knew it is not easy being Russian in independent Latvia, even if you speak the language and were born here. When I first visited in 1993 street signs were in Latvian and Russian. No more. Russians say affirmative action reserves the best jobs for often less-qualified Latvians. Latvians often say they wish the Russians would leave.

Before the € became the Latvian currency Riga was the only place I know where a thin 1 lats coin, the size of a US dime, bought a hamburger and fries at the local McDonald's.

Refreshed from a day of rest, I was eager to get back on the bike. At 11 AM I rode south out of Riga and 24 miles later arrived at Jelgava, the fourth largest city in Latvia.

Ready for a break, I stopped at a grocery store near the town. There I met several teenagers who were out for a ride on this warm sunny day. Two of the girls, Anna and Victoria, spoke

English. They were ethnic Russians and the boys were Latvian. High school students in Jelgava, Anna said they had no trouble speaking Latvian and regarded Latvia as their home country.

We rode off together towards the town. I was astonished to see an elaborate baroque palace, which the riders told me was the Latvian Agricultural University. Later I learned that this sprawling 18th century structure had been the seat of the regional overseer, the duke of Courland, the region encompassing southern Latvia and northern Lithuania. The duke presided over the vast estates of German nobles who dominated Latvia into the 20th century. Jelgava Palace was built in 1737 by the Italian architect who designed the Peterhof and Winter Palace in St. Petersburg.

Subsequently I came across an account by American writer Bayard Taylor who in 1857 traveled 287 miles by stagecoach from St. Petersburg to Jelgava, which at the time was called Mittau.

> *After a journey of three hours from Riga over a sandy plain, we reached Mittau, the ancient capital of Courland. The grand castle, built by Biron, looms over the quiet little town with an air of ostentatious mockery. The Courland nobles, though decayed and fallen, as compared with their former state, are said to be still a proud, chivalric race.*

I was delighted to learn that Taylor's stagecoach rolled along at about the same speed as my bicycle—eight miles per hour—as I too had taken three hours to come from Riga to Jelgava.

Waving farewell to my new acquaintances, I proceeded as a soft rain began to fall. Soon I was back in rural solitude, occasionally seeing in an adjacent field a babushka-clad woman hoeing potatoes. I passed a young boy who used a long stick to make sure the family cow didn't stray from the roadway. Periodically there were dreary two and four story apartment buildings that housed workers from what were collective farms.

By late afternoon, I was uncomfortable from the recurrent rainsqualls that had twice prompted me to put on raingear. My map told me I was approaching the Lithuanian border and a town called Eleja. Perhaps I would be lucky and find a guesthouse. As I came into what was a village and not a town the cyclometer registered 43 miles from Riga. The border was five miles away and I chose not to proceed as my map revealed that I would not soon find a town on the Lithuanian side.

So, as happened twice before, I began looking for a place to stay. Eleja was nothing more than a four corners. There wasn't even a laundromat or bus station. However I found a group of teenagers gathered outside the village store. I inquired if they knew of a place I could stay. The girls giggled and the boys made wisecracks. They paid me no attention and walked away. But a tall blonde girl came back and said in clear English, "perhaps you could stay with us." Her parents were on vacation in Hungary and she and her older brother were in the apartment alone. "Wait," she said, "I'll phone my brother."

Soon 19-year-old Kristaps drove up in a battered car. He was studying computer engineering in Jelgava. His sister Baiba was called Bux. She was 17 and like her brother a student of languages. Bux and I walked to the family apartment not far from the village. It was a three-bedroom apartment on the third floor. There were wide windows that looked out over a field. Bux and Kristaps had their own bedrooms and they agreed that I could stay in the third. Kris had a desktop PC with an internet connection. Bux had a smaller room with a shelf over the bed where her pet white rat Blusa slept in a basket.

After putting my things in the spare room they asked if I would join them at a party that was underway nearby. We drove to another complex where a dozen teenagers were gathered in the community room. Boys sat in straight chairs along one wall with a larger number of girls along the other. Between them was a low table with snacks and soft drinks. Music came from a CD player on the floor. There was little interaction and I felt mildly awkward as if I were attending a junior high dance.

Not long into the evening the one other girl who could speak English rose and stood in the center to announce that the group would like to give me a present. Her name was Linda and she handed me a book entitled "Elejas Pils," or Eleja's Castle. Written in Latvian, German and Russian, it described a castle, the ruins of which we had looked at as we parked the car.

The book was passed around and everyone signed the blank front page. In Latvian, Linda wrote across the top, "A Souvenir from Eleja!" Called Elley in German the grand palace was even larger than Jelgava's and consisted of 19 buildings including a brewery and stables.

Kristaps and Bux, at home in Eleja

That night I slept fitfully—not wanting Blusa the rat, who roamed freely, to pay me a visit. I awoke to find Bux doing dishes, Blusa on her shoulder, as sun streamed in through the window. At the kitchen table adorned with a small bouquet of flowers, the three of us resumed our conversation about Latvia, America and the future. Eventually we took our conversation and tea to the back stoop. Two older women in babooshkas with hoes on their shoulders emerged from the building headed to the potato field across the road.

As we talked, Bux and Kris said what I already surmised,

that Eleja was a boring place that offered no opportunity to young people. Their words confirmed my impression that Latvia was really two countries: vibrant Riga and the impoverished countryside. These young people, whose parents had government jobs, disclosed that there had been a Soviet military base in Eleja as well as a collective farm. Disreputable people, they complained, drug addicts from Riga, were being resettled in Eleja's bleak unoccupied apartments.

Later I learned later that Eleja's military base was a Soviet nuclear missile facility with hidden silos and rockets aimed at Scandinavia and Western Europe.

Our conversation over, I retrieved the bike, left some money with my friends, thanked them profusely and rode off. At the edge of the parking lot a young boy was shooting baskets at a makeshift hoop. The women hoed potatoes in the field. I rode the short distance to the border and effortlessly crossed into Lithuania.

# II.

# LITHUANIA AND KALININGRAD

It was a bright, cool summer morning when I reached Lithuania, the southernmost, most populous Baltic State. The roadway was smooth with wide shoulders. There was little traffic. I was delighted to have come this far.

My target was Siauliai, a medium-sized city in north-central Lithuania, 40 miles straight ahead. Almost imperceptibly the terrain had become undulating hills, a welcome change from the unwavering flatness of Estonia and Latvia.

The ride was uneventful until mid-afternoon when I unexpectedly came upon one of Lithuania's most revered attractions, the Hill of Crosses. Descending a long grade, three tour buses coming from the south turned off the highway onto a secondary road. Reaching the intersection I discovered a sign for a national monument. Having time I decided to follow the buses. Soon there was a virtual sea of crosses spread along the rise of a low hill to the right. Parking and locking the bike, I learned the significance of what had been a makeshift Christian shrine tucked into a rural landscape.

Occupying an expanse equal to several football fields, there were perhaps 200,000 crosses and crucifixes sprouting from the hillside. Visitors moved among them, examining inscriptions.

Guides adept in multiple languages said the practice of placing crosses here began in the mid-19th century as protests to Catholic Lithuania being occupied by orthodox Czarist Russia. During the communist period the Hill of Crosses achieved greater renown because Soviet authorities three times bulldozed the field, only to have the devout arrive by stealth so that in the morning there were even more crosses.

Resuming the journey I regarded the Hill of Crosses as an appropriate introduction and transition from a Protestant northern part of Europe into the Catholic swath that proceeds south and west across Lithuania and Poland.

British historian Alan Palmer writes in his book, *The Baltics*, about the crucial role the Catholic Church has played in Lithuania, the northern bastion of Catholicism. Palmer says because of its shared 300-year monarchy with Poland, Lithuania—unlike Estonia and Latvia—was little impacted by the Reformation. Lithuania's Catholic Church—like Poland's—was instrumental in defeating communism.

Arriving at a pleasant hotel in Siauliai, I spread my maps onto the bed and examined the territory I had traversed. With several peak experiences and nearly 300 miles behind me, I felt satisfaction with the journey thus far. I was also confident that I could carry on all the way to Albania. I realized also that for connecting with people it was better to be on my own. My concerns about safety had been unfounded. With a cell phone in my pocket, not once had I felt myself in danger.

At Siauliai the first leg of my journey was over. I had to return to work and several months went by before I could return to Lithuania. When I was finally able to return, with my boxed bike as accompanied luggage I flew to Klaipeda, Lithuania's port city on the Baltic Sea. My first priority was getting back to Siauliai to resume the journey where I had left off.

At a Klaipeda bike shop I met Saulius Rozinkas, a soft-spoken entrepreneur who had found a niche in bicycle touring. Saulius rents bikes and organizes tours in the Baltic States and the Kaliningrad region of Russia. His clients come mostly from Germany and Holland.

While Saulius and I discussed cycling routes along the Courland Spit into Russia and the unpredictability of riding in the early spring weather, he mentioned that the next day he was traveling by chartered bus to the capital, Vilnius. I was welcome to come with him as he would have the bus drop me closer to Siauliai. This, he said, would be more interesting than traveling from Klaipeda to Siauliai by train. I accepted the invitation.

So on a chilly bright morning in April, Saulius and I joined a dozen young people and clamored aboard a bus, my bicycle stowed in the luggage compartment below. We set out on the modern highway that connects Lithuania's biggest cities—Vilnius, Kaunas and Klaipeda. Once underway Saulius unfolded a map and pointed to back roads he thought I would find appealing. He joked that I would traverse some small hills, "the tallest in Lithuania," he said smiling, knowing that cyclists assume Lithuania is flat.

When we reached the road for Siauliai the driver eased the bus onto the shoulder. He slid the Cannondale out of the luggage compartment. While I organized the load the bus farted a plume of diesel smoke and pulled slowly back onto the highway. The young people and Saulius waved farewell from the rear window. Soon I was alone in the middle of Lithuania.

Here's a simple question. The front carrying rack on a touring bike is built to hold two saddlebags or panniers, one on each side of the front wheel. If you're traveling with a 12-pound load in a single pannier, does it matter whether the load is put on the right side or the left?

That this could become a problem never crossed my mind. What I knew was that since I expected to be riding only two days to get back in Klaipeda, it seemed sensible to have left unneeded baggage in the hotel. Thus I had only rain gear and a change of clothes. I thought I was clever traveling with a single pannier.

Curonian Spit and Kaliningrad

The journey began well. The ride to the first town, Kelme, 18 miles distant, was uneventful. It took two hours, which for me was a normal pace. The weather was superb with a cloudless sky and a temperature of about 50 Fahrenheit. The only negative was a mild easterly wind, the ominous wind from Russia that Peep back in Estonia had warned about.

While taking a break at the Mobil gas station on the edge of Kelme, I wondered why my left knee was hurting. Probably, I thought, it was just a strain from a strenuous game of squash a few days earlier.

At Kelme I made a fateful decision. Following Saulius's suggestion to get off the main road, I gave up on Siauliai and turned left heading northwest into woodlands and fields ready for spring planting. My plan was to connect with the rail line somewhere between Siauliai and Klaipeda and follow it to Klaipeda. Initially it all seemed to work. There was no traffic. Time slowed to a blissful crawl, the only sounds were singing birds and the distant bleating of farm animals. For the first hour I encountered only one person, a woman seeding a large field with a hand planter.

Spring planting, Lithuania

But as the hours slid by I was forced to focus on the persistent, worsening pain from my left knee. Only slowly did I contemplate that the position of the load on the left side of the rack in front of my left leg might be the problem. Was my left knee hurting because it was working harder because of the uneven weight? During a break I shifted the load, attaching it to the top of the rack above the front wheel. The relief was immediate but the damage had been done. It hurt to pedal. Despite my best efforts I was barely advancing.

After a few more miles, I realized I was in trouble. What to do? The train schedule in my pocket revealed that I needed to be at a place called Tryskai Junction where the last train would depart at 8:32 PM. It was already four o'clock.

I was proceeding at less than half my normal speed. The knee hurt more and more. I had 20 miles to go. I did the math. How long would it take? While earlier I thought I'd have an hour to spare at Tryskai Junction, now I wasn't sure.

These were my first moments of despair. Why was I in this predicament? Why was I doing this? I was alone in a remote part of Eastern Europe, in the former Soviet Union no less, didn't speak the language, and this was my vacation! I must be crazy.

The pain became excruciating. I rode ten minutes then walked, which was less painful than pedaling. Maybe there was a bus? Or maybe I could hitch a ride? Silly me, it was Saturday and I hadn't seen *any* vehicle for two hours. The pain worsened. It was getting dark. I gave up hope of making the train.

What should I do? I realized if I didn't get the train my situation would be more desperate than it had been in Estonia or Latvia. Would I be able to find a hayloft or a farm family that would give me shelter? My options were limited. I was in a land of small farms and had already had contentious encounters with angry dogs, although most were chained and unable to give chase. After running all of this through my mind I resolved to go for the train at Tryskai Junction! Be an athlete, I told myself, play through the injury. Just then the hard surface road turned to rutted gravel. I bumped painfully along for another five miles, no longer even sure I was on the right road. My maps were inadequate. This was before Google maps. I navigated by making sure the setting sun was on my left.

I tried pedaling using only my right leg. But even then the bad knee hurt with each turn of the pedal. I passed a village where a sign said 25 kilometers (15 miles) to Tryskai Junction. I had already traveled 40 miles.

Finally I passed a village that my map showed to be near to Tryskai. I scanned the horizon searching for a flat surface on the horizon that would be the rail line. At last, I reached the tracks, crossed them, and turned onto a rutted path that led to the tiny station of Tryskai Junction.

The depot was little more than a shed. From its open window came laughter and the clinking of glasses. When I pushed open the unlocked door the surprised stationmaster gestured to the boyfriend to clear away the glasses and bottle. Her red station-master's cap rested on the signaling device next to the large telegraph key and two rotary phones. Unable to communicate with this unexpected visitor, the young stationmaster pointed to a hand written schedule taped on the wall. It revealed that my timetable was wrong. The last train to Klaipeda had departed several hours earlier.

Moments later the quiet was interrupted by the shrill clanging of the phone, a signal that a train was approaching. The stationmaster positioned the cap on her head, picked up the signaling baton and stepped outside. I followed and watched a train roar past, its wind making us squint and turn away. Back inside the young stationmaster pointed again to the schedule that stated that in 20 minutes, at 8:53 PM, the final train of the day would depart Tryskai for Siauliai.

I didn't know what to do. The bike odometer read 50.3 miles. Discouraged, I switched on the rear light, pushed the bike through the darkness back to the road and looked in all directions. There was nothing, not a house, gas station or store. I was injured, 70 miles from Klaipeda, with nowhere to spend the night. Admitting defeat, I coaxed the bike back up the path to the depot and a few minutes later boarded the train to Siauliai. Seated on a polished wooden bench, I was depressed, aware that I was headed in the opposite direction.

Arriving at Siauliai and feeling better, I checked into a nearby hotel. In the morning I felt better, the knee pain had diminished.

At mid-morning I purchased a $4 ticket and boarded the *Baltias Express* for Klaipeda. Clutching my bike at the far end of the second-class coach, I observed that a red Oriental rug extended along the aisle past rows of unoccupied varnished wooden benches. I stood beneath a brass nameplate that declared the rail car had been refurbished in 1972 in Poznan, Poland.

Amid a driving rain at 10:34 our train swept through Tryskai Junction.

Back in Klaipeda I returned to my hotel and extended my stay. The next morning I was able to move about without difficulty as long as the leg was held straight. But of course I wouldn't be riding. I spent this extra day hobbling about exploring Klaipeda.

For 600 years Klaipeda was German not Lithuanian. Called Memel it was the northernmost outpost of East Prussia. Like Riga it had been part of the Hanseatic League, a transshipment point for products to and from the interior of Czarist Russia.

Memel's name was changed to Klaipeda after the 1919 Versailles Peace Treaty that took the city away from Germany and handed it to the new state of Lithuania. While its majority German population mostly stayed put, inter-ethnic relations grew increasingly tense in the interwar period.

In March 1939 Hitler demanded that the Lithuanians surrender Klaipeda to Germany. They did and its seizure was the dictator's final land grab before the outbreak of the Second World War. Hitler celebrated the triumph by arriving in Memel aboard a battleship. *Time* magazine's correspondent was present when Hitler addressed a wildly enthusiastic crowd that filled Theatre Square.

Aware of the city's complicated history, it is eerie to walk across the empty cobbled square and gaze up at the balcony where Hitler electrified the German masses. I watched as a tour bus of elderly Germans arrived and a guide recounted the story of Hitler and Klaipeda.

Across the square is a museum whose centerpiece is a meticulously crafted scale model of the town from the early 20th century. It fills half the room. The street names are all in German. When you walk outside you witness tangible evidence of the former German presence—particularly the timbered, high gabled facades of 19th century buildings. But when you visit Klaipeda's tourist office the printed materials make little or no mention of the town's German history.

This aside, Klaipeda today is a terrific place, welcoming and prosperous, with a population of 200,000.

What makes Klaipeda important for cyclists is its location at the head of the Curonian or Courland Spit, a 60-mile-long ribbon of sand whose width ranges from a few hundred yards to two miles. These tall, shifting dunes make the spit a place of tranquility and ecological diversity. Beneath tall pines a single roadway weaves between the Baltic Sea and the European mainland. On one side is the windswept sea, on the other a wide still lagoon. Under communism the spit was a closed Soviet military zone. Two-thirds of this pristine refuge is in Lithuania, its southern part in Russia's Kaliningrad province.

The local paper with me and Saulius in Theater Square, the Hitler balcony behind

After a day and a half of rest my knee had recovered. I was eager to ride and get out on the great sand dune. With considerable anticipation on a cold spring morning, I boarded the ferry for the short passage to the spit where I arrived to find only a few people one of whom pointed to a newspaper that featured a photograph of Saulius and me, part of a feature story of a crazy cyclist who was passing through Klaipeda en route to Albania.

The road and trail proceeds in a southwesterly direction, often beneath a canopy of pines. The cycling was swift, the tranquility only occasionally interrupted by the muffled sound of wind through the treetops.

This magnificent dune is the core of Europe's amber coast. Since time immemorial precious resin-like stones have been thrown up from the depths of the Baltic onto the shore. Strollers scour the beach in search of the glinting black and reddish stones, the retrieval of which in times past was the sole domain of the Prussian monarch.

It was a great ride. My destination was Nida, the principal village on the spit. I stopped frequently to check my knee and also just to take in the serene beauty. At times the trail reached towards the lagoon but usually the view was towards the sea.

Midway I stopped to examine a row of polished stones with chiseled Cyrillic letters on the face. It was a memorial to Soviet soldiers who died fighting the Germans who in early 1945 were retreating towards the East Prussian capital, Koenigsberg.

Approaching Nida I observed a solitary wild boar crossing the trail, perhaps 100 yards ahead of me. Stopping, I reached back and removed a video camera from its bag and secured the strap around my neck. I was hopeful I could film this chance encounter with the curious, scary pig-like creature. I rode slowly ahead, my right hand aiming the camera. Reaching the clearing, I was shocked to see not one boar but six to eight of them.

Startled, their heads went up and all eyes were fixed on me. There was a chorus of snorts and two boars pawed the turf, ready to charge. I furiously pushed the pedals and sped off. Only after traveling another hundred yards or so did I look back to confirm that the boars hadn't given chase. My body was trembling. I sang aloud to regain composure and soon met a cyclist approaching from the opposite direction. I signaled for her to stop.

She spoke English and said she was out for an evening ride. I asked whether I should fear wild boars. She assured me I should, that perhaps I had come across a flock that contained babies. Yes, she said, they could have charged and done damage. Thanking her and riding on, I realized just how vulnerable one is on a bike alone in a remote place. I was happy to reach Nida.

The German writer Thomas Mann spent three summers in what the Germans called Nidden. After his first visit in 1930, the Nobel winning novelist purchased property and built a vacation cottage atop Nida's only hill. In visiting the spit Mann and his family joined earlier artists and intellectuals—Richard Wagner and Sigmund Freud, for example—who found summer solace in this most remote part of northern Europe.

Mann was captivated by the tranquil beauty of Nida, as he wrote in a letter to a friend.

> *We spent several days in Nida... and were so impressed that it is truly impossible to write about the uniqueness and beauty of the nature of these environs. ... Here, the sea and the beach are reminiscent of nature's primordial storm.*

Now a museum, Mann's thatched cottage faces inland over the lagoon. When I visited, its clapboard siding, roof, and polished floorboards were newly renovated.

Gazing from the window of Mann's second story study, I too was enchanted by the soft swaying treetops and the still waters of the lagoon beyond.

Mann was an early, vocal critic of Hitler. I find it significant that he chose to build not in the German part of Courland but in Nida, in what at the time was Lithuanian territory. I subsequently learned that after Mann fled Germany his cottage was seized and then used by Goering and others for hunting expeditions. It is haunting to ponder the fate of the books that filled Mann's ground floor library.

Nida, after 70 years of enforced slumber, is again a charming vacation spot, a tranquil refuge where Europe's tribulations seem far away.

Riding on I soon came to the border that today marks the entry not into Germany but Russia.

Of all the places I was traveling, I worried most about Russia; its reputation for lawlessness seemed well deserved. As a makeshift precaution, I had brought with me a letter in Cyrillic Russian explaining who I was and why I was crossing Kaliningrad on a bicycle.

I was the only traveler at the border post. I handed my passport, visa and letter to the female security guard. Reading the latter, she smiled, as if to say that this crazy American has no clue. Her welcoming smile persisted as she handed back the documents and waved me through.

Entering Kaliningrad, Russia

Suddenly I was in Russia, again alone in the middle of nowhere. Would my journey across this Russian exclave be peaceful? Or would I be set upon by bandits springing from the bushes?

Cautiously I rode on. Neither cars nor people were to be seen. Soon the silence was shattered by a crackling of brush in the forest on the seaward side. Through the trees I watched a massive grey elk stroll unevenly through the underbrush, taking no notice of me. I rode on, assured that if elk were my biggest problem I'd be fine. My destination was Zelenogradsk, what was the German resort of Cranz, past Rybachy and Lesnoj, 35 miles dead ahead.

As the miles slipped away, I became aware that the roadway was less well maintained than on the Lithuanian side. Similarly the forest wasn't groomed. Fallen limbs and refuse littered the sand. The few roadside picnic tables were shabby. The infrequent bus shelters were metal skeletons with crude canopies. Trash was often piled next to the roadway. But the serenity of singing birds, the aroma of pine trees, and the gentle lapping of waves on the shore was the same.

After two hours I reached the village of Rybachy (Russian translation, "fishing village") that in German times was called Rossitten. It was a dreadful, rundown place. As I would find everywhere in the Kaliningrad region, many outward signs of the centuries long German presence were defaced. Old single-family dwellings were divided into apartments. Everything was decrepit. Rybachy was a rural slum. Chickens scratched in tall grass and wandered through broken fences. Windows and walls hadn't been painted in years.

Rybachy's streets were unpaved and rutted; uncollected rubbish was piled high. A squat cement community center from communist times was abandoned and looted, shards of glass everywhere. In a forlorn grocery store a woman in a babooshka dispensed a sad selection of breads and meats, plus a greater choice of alcoholic drinks. A few idle men loitered outside smoking and drinking.

Later I learned that the environs of Rybachy harbored something important. When I met him sheltering from a rainsquall and waiting for a bus, Andrey Khalaim, a PhD biologist, was headed to Rybachy's bird sanctuary and scientific station. He had traveled 48 hours by train and bus from St. Petersburg, crossing both Latvia and Lithuania to get to the Russian exclave. Andrey said he would spend two months at the research station run by the Zoological Institute of the Russian Academy of Sciences.

The station has an illustrious pedigree. Occupying several acres on the seaward side, it was established by German ornithologist Johannes Thienemann in 1901 as the world's first banding station for migrating birds. Millions of birds fly overhead annually from as far away as East Africa and the Arctic. Thienemann lived at Rositten for four decades. Carrying on his work, Russian researchers like Andrey band up to 50,000 birds each year.

I asked Andrey about the grim Rybachy village I had visited. Without hesitation he said, "we Russians destroyed everything we touched."

Andrey Khalaim at a bus stop near Rybachy

Bidding the young Russian farewell, I rode on and eventually arrived in Zelenogradsk, a town of 10,000 or so. Cranz was a fashionable resort in German times. But the utter destruction of war and then the privations of communism had turned the place into a ruin that showed only halting signs of renewal. As I rode into town I saw along the beach several Soviet-era hotels, most of them unfinished, some with piles of bricks stacked where they had been left when work was halted. It was the detritus of communism.

Transition must have been a shock for Zelenogradsk. Several once fashionable villas were derelict. Poverty and desolation were dominant impressions. As I rode through the town in search of a hotel, everything was run down.

Soon I came upon a modern structure, the Baltic Crown Hotel. Three stories high with bright lights and tall windows, it was an oasis. Locking the bike outside, I found a fashionably dressed woman who spoke English at the reception desk and used a credit card to pay for the well-furnished room.

War veteran marking Victory Day in Zelenogradsk

I began to relax and lose my fear of being in Russia. I walked to the town center and discovered some modern shops that signaled possible better times. A downtrodden, poorly stocked grocery store in the next block brought me back to the sorry conditions that were the norm in Zelenogradsk. Near the hotel I came upon a war veteran who was looking forward to the celebrations that commemorate the Soviet victory over Nazi Germany.

Refreshed and invigorated, the next morning I looked forward to the short 35-mile ride south to Kaliningrad city. Before departing I purchased a surprisingly detailed map of the province. On the way out of town I passed the newly painted railroad station where a group of young travelers asked to have their picture taken with a visiting cyclist.

Kaliningrad province, the size of Connecticut, is Stalin's gift to Russia. It is war booty, pure and simple. In early 1945 there was fierce fighting as the Red Army steadily advanced. Stalin made clear to his big three cohorts Churchill and Roosevelt that Russia wanted a warm water port on the Baltic and should be compensated for the terrible losses it was suffering. The Potsdam Conference in July 1945 formalized the Soviet and Polish annexation of East Prussia, the biggest territorial change resulting from the war.

Kaliningrad after the collapse of the USSR is an anomaly, separated from Russia proper by two countries and 200 miles. It has no real identity. Its German history has been erased, the German population expelled, while one million Soviet citizens were moved in after the war.

Everything seems out of whack, starting with the name. Mikhail Kalinin was a Stalin loyalist, often referred to by Russians as a party hack. He was a figurehead Soviet president. When he died as the war ended, Stalin borrowed his name to crown this territorial triumph.

Traveling south I chose a back road so I could see the countryside that in German times consisted of vast estates. The riding was easy with no traffic. Along the well-maintained roadway were neat rows of hardwood trees, their lower trunks painted white. I passed an equestrian farm with newly constructed white fences. For a moment I could imagine being in the East Prussia that was renowned for fine horses.

Reaching Kaliningrad city traffic increased and became gridlocked in the center. Recalling my first visit in the mid-1990s, I observed that a submarine that had been opened to visitors was still docked on the Pregel River, but the boat hotel "Hansa" next to it where I had stayed was gone.

There were new hotels and the veneer of the city looked prosperous. Derelict buildings had been spruced up and the landmark Protestant cathedral, restored with German donations, attracted tourists who also visit the grave of Koenigsberg's most famous son, 18th century philosopher Immanuel Kant.

Rural Kaliningrad, a German church now a barn

Still painfully present is the 22-story House of the Soviets, a concrete slab that was to have taken pride of place where the castle of the Prussian kings once stood. Stalin had declared that, "Kaliningrad would have no other history other than that of the Soviet people." The ugly building is called "the monster" by locals.

While Kaliningrad is a relic of the cold war, Koenigsberg, the Prussian city over which it rose, was partially destroyed by British bombing in 1944 that killed 4,500 people.

I met Ivan, a German-speaking Ukrainian, who made a decent living showing visitors around. He carried with him a 1931 map of Koenigsberg, which he carefully unfolds to reveal street names that vanished into history. Inviting me to explore the city with him, Ivan called out the names of long gone buildings and monuments.

We walked the short distance to where Kant's Albertus University once was and paid a few rubles to descend into the city's bunker museum, a principal tourist attraction. Deep beneath the surface in narrow concrete corridors and warrens of tiny rooms the horrors of war became real.

With the Red Army closing in, German commander General Otto Lasch retreated into this bunker that was similar to Hitler's in Berlin. Ordered by the dictator to hold the city at all costs, Lasch fought on and 50,000 Germans and 60,000 Soviets were killed in the fighting. Finally on April 9, 1945, Lasch defied Hitler's orders and surrendered. In a small cubicle is a wax likeness of Lasch seated at the typewriter on which he wrote out the surrender. Receiving the news, Hitler ordered that Lasch and his family be executed as traitors. A month later Hitler was dead and the war over.

Emerging into daylight from the somber scene below ground, modern Kaliningrad appears even more bizarre. I make my way along busy Lenin Prospect where Lenin's statue still occupies a place of honor.

Back at the hotel I loaded my bicycle, ready for the ride south to Poland. But there was one more thing to do. My Russia-born friend in Washington had asked that I visit her aunt and uncle who have lived in Kaliningrad for five decades. Misha (Alexander) had been a Red Army medic during the war. He and his wife Rosa were expecting me. When I arrived at their apartment I was greeted as a long lost friend. That sentiment quickly became mutual.

Alexander (Misha) Sverdlin and Rosa Sverdlina

Misha had just celebrated his 77th birthday. To mark my visit, cakes and other sweets had been spread out on the coffee table in their second-floor walk-up. Seated in an overstuffed chair with white doilies on the arms, Misha deferred to Rosa who showed me family photographs from an album displayed on a glass credenza. I saw pictures of Misha in his uniform, wedding pictures of Rosa and Misha, children, and grandchildren, including my friend Larissa.

A young neighbor was brought in to translate. When I handed Rosa the envelope from Larissa that I knew contained $200, she retreated to the bedroom and returned with tears in her eyes. Rosa was warm and expansive and the love she had for her niece in America was extended to me. Rosa's red hair retained the sheen of her youth. More than once she embraced me with the same affection that I remembered from my own mother.

As time passed, twice I was overcome with emotion and wept openly. I can't explain why but it was a visceral recognition of shared humanity, a personal connection to a time before the cold war I had grown up with when Americans and Russians had a common purpose. No doubt I was also reacting to the poignant stories I had recently heard, the visit to the ruins of war, all of that pent-up emotion spilled out during my time with the Sverdlins.

It must also be true that there are similarities between Russians and Americans, an observation I've heard often from East Europeans. Peep back in Estonia had said, "You're both from big countries and you both think in big terms and come up with big projects. Russians," he said, "like Americans are expansive, generous and friendly. And you're both used to being dominant."

During long hours of riding I had thought often about the Russians as displaced hegemons, aware of just how much they had lost when after 1989 all of Stalin's gains in Eastern Europe were given up, often without shots being fired. The opening of the Berlin Wall brought welcome freedom to millions, including later on Russians themselves. But so far on this journey I had witnessed the petty humiliations Russians were forced to endure in parts of their former empire. One instance stands out. On my first visit to Kaliningrad in 1995 I was a passenger on a bus traveling to Klaipeda. At the border crossing the Lithuanian guards collected all the passports, but only the Russians were ordered off for further inspection. To me it was needless payback for past horrors. How would we Americans comport ourselves under similar circumstances?

All that Misha and Rosa once believed in was gone and discredited. And while they cherished the new freedoms, the role of the state had been reduced and they had to make do more on their own. They were delighted that the communist experiment was over but bewildered by the changes. "What can we do?" said Misha. "We don't know what will happen." When I asked why the old Soviet names like Lenin and Kalinin were still used, Misha waved a dismissive hand, "it's our history, the only one we've got." When I asked about the war, he said it was horrific and too painful to discuss.

Emotionally spent, I declined my hosts' invitation to lunch and probably too quickly departed, as only then was I offered the traditional Slavic welcome of bread and salt, which I awkwardly consumed.

Why, I've often thought, was I so impacted by my brief time with the Sverdlins? It was, I think, because suddenly and unexpectedly I found myself face to face with the human side of epic conflict. I was undone by their basic humanity, of being their honored guest. Rosa in her apron, showing me photos from her album, saying more than once, "it is such a wonderful family."

Gathering myself, I made my way outside, inspired by Misha and Rosa.

And with that I rode off with regret in my heart, deeply grateful that I had come to Kaliningrad province and ridden across it. I was glad I had not yielded to fear. Kaliningrad, without doubt, was the most interesting place I had yet visited.

Riding straight south, in less than three hours I arrived at the Russian Polish border where traffic was backed up. To the Russian authorities I produced my folded letter of introduction along with my passport. A stern border guard read it, looked at me and then my bicycle, smiled broadly, and waved me through.

Bagrationvsk, leaving Kaliningrad

# III.

# POLAND

Travelers reaching Poland from the west invariably observe that the country is relatively poor compared to western Europe. The lingering effects of four decades of communism are still visible. But entering Poland from the north as I did from Kaliningrad Russia, one gets a different perspective.

After threading through traffic at the Bagrationovsk border crossing and entering Poland, I felt I had arrived in the west. Figuratively, it was like walking from a dimly lit room into daylight. The difference was immediate and pronounced. Now farm buildings were painted. There were fresh road signs and markings, brush near the shoulders had been cleared away, villages had sidewalks, people were better dressed.

After the emptiness of rural Kaliningrad, Poland was busy and relatively crowded. With a population of approaching 40 million, Poland is eight times more populous than the three Baltic States and Kaliningrad combined.

After two hours of uneventful riding, I reached Lidzbark Warminski, a town 20 miles from the border and 48 miles from Kaliningrad city. As with Kaliningrad, this part of Poland was German East Prussia. For most of its history Lidzbark Warminski was Heilsberg and the older buildings are recognizably German.

Geographically I was 110 miles north of Warsaw at the edge of the Masurian lake country. Hitler's Wolf's Lair, the dictator's headquarters in East Prussia (where he barely escaped assassination in 1944), was not far away. That site attracts occasional visitors but I had neither time nor interest to see it.

Unwittingly I had arrived on a holiday weekend and the hotels in Lidzbark Warminski were full. A pizza deliveryman on a motorbike directed me to a motel south of town. Thanking him, I rode on hoping for good luck. Darkness was approaching and I was ready to stop. Soon I arrived at a gabled structure on the side of a hill set back from the road. Seeing a German tour bus in the parking lot my spirits sank as its presence probably meant every room was taken. Ascending the hill I eyeballed the bus as possible accommodation, aware that my exhausted legs were telling me that I wasn't riding to the next town.

Entering the lobby, a thin youngish man hurried in from the dining room where he was putting down place settings for the evening meal. Speaking English, he said he was the owner, and yes all the rooms were taken. Plaintively I explained my predicament and raised the question of whether I might sleep on the bus. The proprietor, whose name was Tomasz, thought for a moment and said I could have the unoccupied maid's room just off the lobby. The price was reasonable. I was delighted. The small room was clean and more than adequate. I joined the tour group for a supper of soup, sausage, potatoes, Riesling wine, and pudding.

At the meal I was placed next to a physician from Kassel. He told me the bus would travel to Kaliningrad the next day and that his ancestral roots were in the former East Prussia. He wished to see where his family once lived. When I told him I had come from Kaliningrad, he remarked that the Poles were lucky compared to the Russians.

I was puzzled by his comment, so he explained. "Through four decades of communism," he said, "the Poles had the Catholic Church as an institutional anchor. Their farms were never taken away or collectivized as in other communist lands." The Russians, he continued, had to endure communism for 30 years longer than the Poles and had neither religion nor land to hold on to. He concluded, "we often forget that serfdom continued in Russia almost to the time of Lenin's 1917 revolution." While my German acquaintance's analysis was interesting, I said that I was sure Poles saw things differently, comparing themselves not with Russians but with Germans and others to the west.

In the morning after the tour bus departed, Tomasz and I sat down and talked over a cup of coffee. He expounded on Poland's flourishing small business sector of which he was proudly a part. Entrepreneurship came naturally to Poles, he said, and he offered his own story as typical.

While still in his teens, he said, he worked several years in western Germany, saving money and learning the language.

After returning home he got married and then borrowed from the bank to buy the motel. Tomasz was a textbook example of the new generation of Poles moving up the economic ladder. His generation is determined to catch up with the west and live the normal life that was unavailable to their parents and grandparents. The previous evening I had observed Tomasz's fluent German, his attentiveness to customers, and his efficient manner that elicited praise from guests. As we parted, Tomasz said, "the accident of geography requires that we Poles and Germans get along."

Hoeing potatoes, northern Poland

Back on the bike, I rode in a westerly direction over secondary roads towards the larger town of Elblag. I was surprised to find the Polish countryside relatively crowded both with traffic and settlements. Small farmhouses dotted the landscape and I had to watch out for tractors and trucks coming out of the fields. Again I was comforted that the orange safety flag waved from my rear rack. On this first full day in Poland, I rode 55 miles through woodlands and farms before arriving in Elblag.

I checked into a downtown hotel and a comfortable room that looked out over the tall spire of a gothic-style church in the main square. As I took in this lovely panorama, I pondered the physician's words of the previous night and thought back to distant Latvia and the castles of the ruling gentry. It hadn't occurred to me that most Latvians were descended from landless peasants.

The next town was Malbork where I sought out a bike shop because my chain was slipping. In German times Malbork was Marienburg, famed for its sprawling medieval castle said to be largest brick structure in Europe. Across the way from the ramparts there was a hardware store where a man was arranging an outdoor display of mowers and garden equipment. Pushing the bike across the street I pointed to my chain and asked if there was a bike shop nearby. To my surprise the man answered in English, "let me have a look." Fetching a wrench from inside he returned to skillfully adjust the rear derailleur. Minutes later the bike was fixed. When I asked the price, the young Pole waved a dismissive hand and said payment would not be accepted. It was a magnanimous gesture of the kind I found repeatedly on my journey.

Territory taken from Germany in 1945. My route in dashed line.

While surveying the beauty of Malbork, it was obvious from the old buildings that this too had been German. At the Potsdam Conference in July 1945 Britain and the U.S. acceded to Stalin's demand that Poland be physically moved 150 miles west. Polish lands in the east became part of the Soviet Union and the Poles displaced there were sent to the lands from which five million Germans were expelled. East Prussia meanwhile was divided between Russia and Poland.

Examining an old map, I realized that about half of my route through Poland traversed lands that were once part of Germany.

My bike now in good repair, I rode seven hours through intermittent rain that day and traveled 43 miles. By evening I reached the depressed industrial town of Grudziadz where I spent the night. Grudziadz lies on the east bank of the Vistula, Poland's principal north flowing river that rises way to the south in the Polish heartland. Asking an elderly man for directions to a hotel, he immediately complained about the city's 30% unemployment rate and the closure of a big tire factory. "At least under communism," he said, "everybody had a job, unlike today."

Grudziadz was grimy and uninviting. The next day there was partial sun and I rode again over back roads south along the Vistula. For the first time, I picked up a riding companion. Twenty-two-year-old Gregorz Jonutowski, an economics student at nearby Torun University, rode with me for about six miles. He had drawn up alongside near his home village. He was en route to his grandmother's and wished to practice his English. Gregorz hadn't traveled abroad but looked forward to doing so. He had a personal computer at home. He had run two marathons and was looking forward to the Tour de Poland, a cycling race that would soon take place in this vicinity.

That evening at half past six I reached the pleasant city of Bydgoszcz. In seven hours of riding I had traveled 49 miles.

Bydgoszcz sported a downtown pedestrian mall that was

both handsome and abundant in the shops and goods that were on offer. A street accordionist played 1940s dance-era favorites. There were modern bakeries and shops of the kind found in Berlin or Paris.

At my hotel I examined my progress. I had come 90 miles in two days, traveling byways never far from the Vistula. Somewhere, I'm not sure precisely where, I had crossed from historical Germany into Wielko Polska, Great Poland, the Polish heartland where Poles have always comprised a majority.

Cycling in Poland you observe a nation on the move. There is a palpable vitality. People seemed determined to pick themselves up and build. Poles are active, whether painting their homes or working the fields late into the evening. They are prolific traders, buying and selling everything from cars to consumer goods sold in makeshift markets. Nowhere except in Albania have I witnessed such spontaneous entrepreneurship.

From the seat of a bicycle a rider has six to eight hours each day simply to think and contemplate the world. I found myself imagining what it was like in Poland during the hard days of communism in the 1980s. I remembered that it was in Gdansk, not far from Malbork, where Lech Walesa organized the shipyard revolt that led to the Solidarity movement that ultimately brought down communism.

Riding on I thought of Poland's tragic history and its literal disappearance for nearly 150 years. From 1772 until 1919 Polish lands were occupied by rival imperial powers—Germany, Russia and Hapsburg Austria. Perhaps it is because of that cruel history that tenacity, resistance and perseverance are so engrained in Polish character.

Pushing deeper into the country, I came to Gniezno, the lovely cathedral town between Poznan and Bydgoszcz that was the capital of medieval Poland. In Gniezno I was told the legend of three Slavic brothers—Lech, Cech and Rus—who had supposedly been hunting in the wilds of central Europe. They went off in three directions, goes the tale, with Lech following a white eagle north to its home in Gniezno (which means 'nest'). Lech is said to have founded in Gniezno the Polish nation. Rus went east, founding Ukraine and Russia. And to the south Cech founded the Czech lands of Bohemia and Moravia. Gniezno remains the heart of Polish Catholicism and the white eagle is the Polish national symbol.

The next day on a cold morning I rode out from Gniezno. While still on city streets I was treated to a disappearing urban tableau that has been a fixture of life for centuries. Parked on the street in front of me was an aging flatbed truck. From beneath its dirty tarpaulin a wiry man bent under the weight of a canvas backpack laden with black coal. Gazing quickly in both directions, the man darted across the road and disappeared into a narrow passage separating two large buildings.

Entranced by this unexpected sight, I parked the bike and watched curling plumes of coal smoke rise from narrow rooftop chimneys in the structure the coalman entered. Minutes later the wiry man, carrying the empty rucksack, emerged from the passage and returned to the truck for another load.

Fixated on what for the people of Gniezno was routine, I breathed in the pungent aroma of soft coal smoke. Before pedaling on I watched the blackened deliveryman in his overalls complete another delivery. Engrossed in his work the coalman had taken no notice of the bicycle or its rider.

Still in the far reaches of Gniezno, I came upon two very young boys pulling a wagon piled high with tree branches and brush they had scavenged along the roadside. Their load would be kindling for lighting the home fire.

By now my Polish journey had evolved into a kind of personal epiphany. I confess that until this extended visit to Poland I wasn't enamored with the country. Perhaps it was my midwestern Protestant upbringing and ingrained skepticism of devout Catholicism. I've had a hard time pronouncing Polish words and found spoken Polish less appealing to the ear than the Czech that I knew from living three years in Prague. But now I admired the Poles, their courtesy, good humor and work ethic that was so clearly apparent.

Observers of Poland know there is an extraordinary bond between Poles and the Catholic Church. While communists frowned on constructing churches during their 40 years in power, hundreds have been built since 1989. New houses of worship are everywhere and Sunday mass brings out not just the old but also the young. The immensity of pride Poles feel for the village priest who became Pope is reflected in seemingly every town having a Jana Pavlova II (John Paul II) street. John Paul became Pope 11 years before communism ended and there can be little doubt that his stature as the Pole leading the world's Catholics hastened communism's demise. His presence—living in freedom in Rome—was a powerful message to Poles that oppressive communism was not permanent. John Paul II embodied the traits Poles hold dear—courage, loyalty, dignity, and generosity.

I was now riding south and west from Gniezno, skirting Poznan, Poland's fifth largest city. On this day I thought of the stark contrasts between old and new. There is an extraordinary revival in Polish agriculture—big John Deere tractors are replacing the ubiquitous Ursus machines from communist days. But despite modernity you still see people working the fields with hand tools and animals.

Impressed by the progress I was witnessing, I thought of that time not that long ago when Poland was an economic basket case. In the mid-1980s Mikhail Gorbachev's perestroika and glasnost were in full bloom and throughout Eastern Europe communist rigidities were bending. But at that time Poland lagged economically. By the time the Berlin Wall came down in 1989 Poland had descended into economic dysfunction with shortages of basic goods and runaway inflation.

But when Poland's first non-communist government took power things quickly turned around. The courageous decisions to turn off the printing press, open up the closed economy, and allow prices and wages to be set by market forces were the core of Poland's "big bang" transformation. It quickly became a model for other east bloc countries set free from the collapsing Soviet Union.

Amid these reflections I thought of my journalist friend in Warsaw who had observed that "under communism people were like animals in the zoo, guarded and penned up." Now, she said, for better or worse "the zoo is gone and the people are free to move about in the jungle." Her use of the word jungle to describe Poland's new market economy was deliberate.

I rode on and crossed the east-west freeway connecting Warsaw and Berlin. Twelve miles farther on I reached the small town of Sroda.

In late afternoon after another 12 miles, I reached Srem, which I learned is famous for its ironworks and foundry that produces church bells. In the outskirts I passed what appeared to be a large community picnic. I diverted from the roadway to have a look. While riding slowly among the hundreds of spectators, a young dad towing a child carrier behind his bike drew up beside me. Speaking little English but some German, he said his name was Stefan Barkoviak. He called himself an avid cyclist and wanted to know about my trip.

After some minutes' conversation Stefan invited me to stay overnight with his family. Caught off guard, I couldn't say no. Soon, with his sleeping son in tow, we pedaled off into the town and Stefan's apartment complex.

After 15 minutes we reached a typical three-story communist-era housing bloc. From the parking lot Stefan shouted up to his wife who was standing next to a second floor window. He asked her to set another place for supper and she smiled approvingly. Having parked our bikes we went upstairs where I met

Stefan's wife and an 11-year-old son who was busy playing computer games. After brief conversations, we sat down to a wonderful meal of golabki, the Polish specialty of rolled cabbage, meat and rice.

Me, Stefan and his infant son at the Srem sport grounds

Later, seated on the couch beneath the portrait of Jesus that is a fixture in many Polish homes, Stefan told me he worked irregularly in web design and advertising. Sport, he continued, was his passion and he typically cycled 2,000 miles each year. That evening we made an excursion to the sport center of the iron foundry, where a dozen friends were enjoying beer and conversation after bowling. Friendship banners from the communist period adorned wood-paneled walls. There were display cases filled with mementoes—stickers, decals and signed photos from the 1970s and '80s that proclaimed solidarity with sporting clubs in East Germany.

Back at Stefan's apartment, I was given the living room sofa. Delighted but exhausted, I tallied the day's total as I spread a few belongings over the borrowed duvet. I had been on the road seven hours and traveled 42 miles from Gniezno.

At 9:30 the next morning, thanking my hosts, I rode off to the southwest towards the German border, which I now calculated to be only two days away. I was currently directly south of Poznan and about two-thirds of the way across Poland.

By early afternoon I had traveled 24 miles and reached the substantial town of Leszno. While shopping for snacks on the main street I came upon a brochure in English that explained that with its favorable winds Leszno was a valued locale for aerial gliding. When I stepped outside I observed a glider circling high in the sky and realized that I had stumbled onto an international gliding competition. When the road west passed the airport I paused to watch the aerial feats. I could have tarried longer but my map told me that I needed to travel 36 more miles by nightfall.

After four more hours crossing rural Poland I reached a bridge over River Oder. This was my introduction to the town of Glogow or Glogau. During the 53-mile ride from Srem I had crossed from Wielko Polska back into what was German Silesia.

In German times Glogau was a way station between Berlin and Breslau, the Silesian capital to the southeast of where I was. Breslau is now Wroclaw. Glogau in German times had been the headquarters of Carl Flemming Publishers, a world-renowned printer of maps and atlases. As a bibliophile I knew that name well and had wanted to visit Glogau. Each time I unfolded my prized 1869 railway map of Europe I was intrigued by the mysterious imprint, 'Carl Flemming Verlag, Glogau.' Alas not a trace of the publishing house survived World War II. Glogow was essentially destroyed in 1945 when the Germans sought in vain to block the Red Army's advance towards Berlin.

I checked into the Qubus Hotel and there met Magdalena, a young hotel clerk who when her shift ended took me on a walking tour. As with Warsaw's old town Glogow's historic center has been meticulously reconstructed. We visited a charming old town pub with rough-hewn beams, overstuffed easy chairs, a good selection of European beers, and soft sounds of American jazz.

Returning to the hotel, I settled in for a good night's sleep in what I imagined would be my last night in Poland. I found myself thinking of Chopin, the extraordinary 19th century composer who in his way is as central to Polish identity as Pope John Paul II. I remembered our family visit to Warsaw in 1995 where we attended the Chopin Piano Competition that takes place every five years. A highlight was visiting Chopin's birthplace 30 miles west of the capital.

Dying at age 39 in distant Paris at the height of his fame and cut off from his homeland, Chopin exemplifies the romantic patriot, the tragic hero so central to Polish identity. Global strategist George Friedman writes this about the composer:

> To understand Poland, you must understand Frederic Chopin...In the Revolutionary Etude, written in the wake of an uprising in Warsaw in 1830 crushed by Russian troops, there is both rage and resignation... [Leaving his homeland shortly thereafter] Chopin never returned..., but Poland never left his mind...Listen carefully to Chopin: Courage, art and futility are intimately related for Poland. The Poles expect to be betrayed, to lose, to be beaten. Their pride was in their ability to retain their humanity in the face of catastrophe.

So, I wondered, what differentiates Poland from the other lands in Eastern Europe? Is it its tragic history? Being bigger and more populous than its neighbors? Being so demonstrably Catholic in a sea of atheists? Or its stunning economic success?

Poland's foreign minister in the millennium years was Radek Sikorski, a brilliant scholar and journalist turned politician who was educated at Oxford. Fervently anti-communist and conservative, Sikorski at the age of 48 in early 2011 delivered a bold speech in parliament asserting that these were the best years ever in Poland's long and tangled history. Defending himself against charges of being subservient to the European Union or the United States, Sikorski spoke these words to opposition lawmakers:

> ...*Come to your senses! And understand that today's Poland — which is founded on democratic and free-market values, which we all sought in our own ways, where many wrongs are still unaccounted for, and which is still far from ideal — is the best Poland we have ever had. Learn to love it!*

Is this the best time ever for Poland? Perhaps. Poland is a member of NATO and the European Union and plays an active, constructive role in both. Because of the horrors of the Second World War and Holocaust, Poland is essentially a mono-ethnic state, bereft of its Jews and Germans, groups with which it seldom had good relations.

At 11:00 the next morning I set out from Glogow for what I expected to be a long and challenging ride, hoping that by nightfall I would reach the River Neisse and cross into Germany. Little did I know just how long and challenging the day would be.

From the previous day's ride I had concluded that in south-western Poland things were somewhat askew. Signposts were often confusing. I was convinced that without knowingly traveling on a main road it was very easy to get lost.

Compared to elsewhere in Poland this region felt curiously remote. It was less crowded as well. My maps presented conflicting data—varying road numbers and even different place names with inconsistent placement of villages.

From the beginning things went badly. Incredibly, I took the wrong road out of Glogow, heading *northwest* instead of south-west over route 12, my intended route. There were no markings at all and I merely followed the flow of traffic. After 15 minutes

I sensed something was wrong. Traffic had disappeared and the surface of the tarred road was now potholed. There were no signs. Looking at the sky, the sun was not where it should be. My maps were useless.

This was the first time that I was lost.

Aware that things weren't right, I didn't know what to do. I rejected the idea of turning back as that would take too much time. Better, I thought, to continue on until I reached a village where there would be signs and I could get my bearings.

Soon I reached a hamlet where a forlorn sign declared "Zukowice." One map said I was three miles *northwest* of Glogow.

There was an unused railroad crossing and beyond it a village church where I stopped to study my maps and make a plan. I resolved to go forward even though doing so was venturing further into the unknown. I had come too far to turn back. One map suggested I would eventually reach a bigger road that would lead to Zagan, my initial destination.

Climbing back on the bike, I noticed a gravestone and marker in the churchyard where I had rested. I pushed the bike over to the marker and read a German language inscription. "Hier ruht in Gott, Juliana Maslack," it stated, "gb. Jung 22.10 1847 4-6-1943." Here rests in God Juliana Maslack, born in 1847, died in 1943 (the year of my birth). At least here in western Poland, I thought, unlike in Kaliningrad, German graves had been left intact and not desecrated.

I set out from Zukowice aware that the day would be hard with an uncertain outcome. After another hour I reached the larger village of Bytom Ordanksa, which my 1:700 000 scale Michelin map told me was 12 miles northwest of Glogow. For the first time on this journey, I realized, I was navigating by the seat of my pants over back roads that at times were little more than trails. There were few signs and fewer people. I hadn't found the bigger roads promised on one of my maps. The landscape had become sandy and forested.

Windmill in rural Poland

I pressed on. The weather was good and while I felt no danger, I was utterly alone. Steadily I proceeded and came eventually to Styputow, a run-down village north of Zagan. The tarred road became cobblestone. The few buildings were brick. Some were abandoned. After another hour, there were signs of life. There was an apple orchard and finally I entered Zagan. At its north end a formidable tall fence like those in the concentration camps enclosed the town cemetery. Venturing inside through an open gate, I found graves of German soldiers from World War I.

Finally I had reached Zagan where I again studied my maps. Now the question was what route should I follow to the German border. I was unsure which of two border crossings I should target. Should I aim for the crossing that was marked as secondary, to be used only by Germans and Poles? That one at Przewoz, three maps agreed, was not an international crossing. Would I be allowed to cross? On the Michelin map Przewoz was so inconsequential that it warranted only the smallest type-face. Would I even be able to find it? At this point, truth be told, I was lost.

I chose to ride southeast from Zagan on a secondary road carved through a pine forest. One map indicated that this was a protected area, perhaps a national park. Proceeding, I came to a clearing where two cars were parked near what appeared to be a recently constructed guard tower. I diverted into the clearing and discovered members of a British film crew preparing a doc-umentary on a World War II prisoner of war camp situated at this place. Only then did I learn that I had stumbled onto Stalag Luft III, the scene of The Great Escape.

It was here, only 100 miles southeast from Berlin, where up to 10,000 captured airmen—mostly British, Canadian and American—were held as prisoners. As the camp was admin-istered by the Luftwaffe, the captives—virtually all of them officers—were permitted a wide range of activities, including sports. Aware of likely escape attempts, the Germans had sit-uated the camp where the soil was sandy and presumably inca-pable of supporting tunnels. Nonetheless, over a six-month period the airmen constructed three 100-yard-long tunnels 30 feet beneath the ground. They called the tunnels Tom, Dick and Harry.

From the film crew I learned that on a moonless night in March 1944, nearly 300 of the imprisoned pilots descended into the tunnels. Because an alarm had been sounded, only 73 actu-ally emerged into the forest beyond the prison perimeter. Of these only three—two Norwegians and a Dutchman—reached freedom. Two made it to Sweden, the other to Spain. Hitler ordered that the rounded up escapees be executed. Unlike in

Film crew and cyclist at Stalag Luft III near Zagan

the iconic 1963 movie a motorcycle did not carry the Steve McQueen figure to freedom.

After a fascinating hour hearing the story and exploring the few remains of the camp, I remounted and rode deeper into the pine forest, hoping that I would find the way to the border before dark. Still without a good regional map, I turned into unmarked lanes that I hoped corresponded to what I saw on the Michelin map. Only when I reached a village with signposts—in this case Wymiarki—did I know I was right. After another 90-minute ride I reached the German border at the village of Przewoz (Priebus) on the north-flowing Neisse River. On the Polish side there were few people but one kind person pointed me toward the border. Luckily without formalities or inspection I was waved across the narrow bridge into eastern Germany.

By now I had come 910 miles from Tallinn and was almost halfway to Albania, my ultimate destination. I had traversed five countries—Estonia, Latvia, Lithuania, Russia, and Poland. I had averaged from 42 to 53 miles on each day of riding.

Typically I was in the saddle about eight hours per day. I seldom began before 10 AM.

In Poland I had traveled 320 miles in six days, averaging 53 miles per day. My average speed was 12 miles per hour.

Significantly, the trip thus far had been without incident. There were no accidents, thefts or big mishaps. Yes, some boys in a Polish village had thrown firecrackers at me that went off loudly but harmlessly beneath the bike. A truck had crumpled my sunglasses that had fallen to the pavement near Bydgoszcz. I had lost my U lock but replaced it.

My biggest error was the wrong turn out of Glogow. That mistake cost me 12 extra miles and at least an extra hour of riding. But in the larger scheme of things all this was minor. Having reached Germany, I felt confident that physically I could do the trip. Yes, the terrain thus far had been mostly flat and the mountains lay ahead. But I would manage.

# IV.

# GERMANY
## AND THE CZECH REPUBLIC

My arrival from Poland at the Priebus border crossing was anticlimactic. Contrary to expectations there was no village on the German side and there was nothing in the vicinity. The border guard said I needed to ride 12 miles south to Rothenburg to find accommodation.

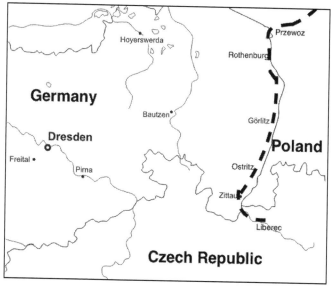

The ride along the River Neisse in Saxony, eastern Germany

It was 8:30 PM and nearly dark. I was exhausted after a 59-mile ride through western Poland. The exhilaration of reaching Germany instantly became dismay at having to keep riding. But there was no other option.

I set off on a dark stretch of a well-maintained roadway. The night sky was black and I had no headlight as I falsely assumed I would not be riding at night. Only the flashing red taillight announced my presence on a lonely two-lane road.

From time to time a line of trees to the east told me I was close to the river. Having observed at the border crossing that the Neisse was little more than a stream, I wondered why Winston Churchill made such a big deal about the Oder-Neisse line at wartime conferences. The rivers had never formed a frontier and Stalin's land grab deprived Germany of 23% of its pre-World War II territory. At Yalta in February 1945 Churchill said to Stalin, "it would be a pity to stuff the Polish goose so full of German food that it got indigestion."

At 9:30 PM I reached Rothenburg, a tidy town more prosperous than those I had visited on the Polish side. Riding past closed food markets and shops, I eventually reached the nearly deserted town square. Only on a far corner were there lights. It was a beer garden that was still open. Asking about accommodation a friendly waitress directed me to an unlit restaurant across the way whose owner, she said, ran a guesthouse.

Locking the bike and venturing inside, the man was already sweeping up and preparing to go home. Yes, he said, there was a room available for €10. I handed over the money and he handed me a large metal ring with two keys, one for the building, one for the second floor room. Escorting me outside he pointed to the large unlit building two doors away.

It was totally dark but I managed to get the oversized key into the lock and the tall wooden door creaked open. With no flashlight or match to locate an interior light, I crept up the cement stairs. I was the only guest. Finding the room, I collapsed into the bed, not remembering until morning his instructions for turning on the gas and water.

I awoke with sunlight streaming through the window. I reached for the maps that lay on the floor and surveyed the previous day's progress. I had logged 72 miles and been in the saddle for ten hours. Now I really did feel exhilaration.

Refreshed, I went downstairs in search of breakfast. I found a bakery for croissants and coffee. Then I walked across the square and through the town. Rothenburg was lovely but eerily quiet. Buildings were newly painted. There were red geraniums in most second story window boxes.

Beyond the square were the accoutrements of modern life—a post office, school, clinic, bank, pharmacy and two more restaurants. Everything was new or recently renovated. A new but empty regional bus glided past. Down the hill behind the square the north-flowing Neisse slid lazily by.

But on closer inspection, it was apparent that Rothenburg had problems. Where were the people? A hotel on the far side of square was closed. Several shops were closed. Two teenage boys sat on a bench drinking beer. They said they were unemployed and had nothing to do.

Stopping at a convenience store on the edge of town, I was told the brightest young people had left for Munich or Berlin as there were no jobs here. Rothenburg's population had declined since unification and the jobless rate exceeded 20%. Thus in this corner of old East Germany there was the veneer of modernization but little activity.

In the town park I found the secluded bike trail adjacent to the Neisse that I would follow south to the Czech border. The morning ride was idyllic as I was the only cyclist on a serene wooded trail.

Having enjoyed the beauty of Rothenburg, I thought about the immense changes that had occurred in eastern Germany since unification in 1990. In western Germany there are complaints about the billions spent to modernize the east, but I think the money has been well spent. I saw firsthand the newly paved roads, sidewalks, telecommunications links, regional transport, and upgraded public services.

I had seen with my own eyes that East Germany before unification was a gray, unwelcoming place. I spent a week in the German Democratic Republic in March 1990 writing articles for the *Financial Times* and *Los Angeles Times*. I vividly recall that in Weimar, the city of Goethe, Schiller and Buchenwald, there were only three hotels where foreigners could stay and they were fully booked. I was saved by a newly established tourist agency—an incipient Airbnb—that sent visitors into private homes. Today, by contrast, Weimar sparkles and is utterly transformed, unrecognizable from what it was under communism.

As I rode on I came to Gorlitz where the trail ascended a steep slope from the river up into the town. Gorlitz is often described as the most picturesque place in Germany. Since the Neisse is an international border, the eastern part of the city is now Zgorzelec, Poland and the twin towns are often presented as a model of European Union cooperation.

That evening I arrived in Ostritz, a village several miles south where the Neisse is narrow and a simple footbridge connects Germany with Poland. Stopping, I watched a red Deutsche Bahn train engine glide slowly along on the Polish side. This seemed odd until I discovered that the German rail line and the Ostritz station are actually in Poland.

I stopped at the Hotel Neisseblick, a complex of three buildings within the compound of an old factory. In communist times, I learned, this had been a textile enterprise that made clothing and employed 1,500 workers. Settling into a small, comfortable room with television and internet, I regarded the Neisseblick as a pleasant farewell to my short journey through Germany.

At breakfast in the morning, the only other guest was a tall, swarthy-complexioned man who said he was returning to his

Ostritz, Germany

home near Munich from a nostalgic trip back to the place in Poland where he spent his childhood. His name was Hermann Pratz and he spoke impeccable English.

Hermann was a sprightly man in his 70s. He had spent the previous day at what had been his family estate near Leszno, Poland, the very place where I had stopped to watch the gliders.

Hermann Pratz in Ostritz

Twelve when the war ended, Pratz told me how in February 1945 as the Russians approached, his family fled west. "Because there was no fuel," he said, "we traveled with horses and wagons trying to get away from the Russians." He remembered that as the refugee caravan neared Dresden he watched the horrific nighttime bombings that killed up to 25,000 people and destroyed much of the city that was known as the Venice of the north. Pratz continued, "the sky turned absolutely red. It was like the northern lights except red. We also could hear the rumble from the explosions." He and his family eventually reached Munich, the Bavarian city that became home to thousands of Germans displaced from the east. The war ended, Pratz grew up, studied geophysics and made his career in the West German patent office.

It was gripping to hear this eyewitness account of the Dresden firebombing, an event that I knew about from Kurt Vonnegut's *Slaughterhouse Five*. Vonnegut, a young G.I., had been captured in the Battle of the Bulge and was a POW in Dresden at the time of the bombing. Amazingly, he survived but his group of prisoners had the gruesome task of collecting the bodies of civilians, most of whom had died of asphyxiation. Listening to Pratz, I recalled that in the mid-90s while I was living in Prague—80 miles south of Dresden—two elderly neighbors said they too saw the nighttime sky turn red. They said they would never forget what they saw.

Like many Germans displaced from the east, Pratz would like to purchase the former family homestead from its Polish owners. He had been politely received on his visit, he said, but he thought a deal unlikely. "They [the Poles] don't want us back," he said. Turning sentimental, Pratz reflected, "it's amazing, as I drove near the old place I didn't need a map, I knew every road and lane from memory." He regretted that his Polish language skills, unused since childhood, were rudimentary.

Later that morning Pratz and I learned from the hotel owner that what is now the Neisseblick was until 1990 an active factory. Unable to survive the transition to a free market, the enterprise was closed and a family from Frankfurt bought everything for $140,000. They then invested over $1 million to convert the factory into an attractive hotel. The owner complained that tourism had failed to grow as projected and that German businesses were leapfrogging Ostritz to put their money into Poland where wages were lower.

Enriched from these stories, I set out at noon still proceeding south on the bike path along the River Neisse. My target was the Czech city of Liberec.

As I rode, the terrain above the bike path became wooded and I had entered a range of low mountains. I passed Zittau, the southernmost German town situated in rolling country where the borders of Poland, the Czech Republic and Germany meet. Seeking to avoid a busy highway border crossing, my maps showed a footpath that crossed into Czech Bohemia. When I couldn't find it, I asked directions and was sent off across a field to where a hiking trail led off into the woods.

After several minutes of searching and seeing no one, my doubts were dispelled. Ahead was a signpost bearing the lion of Bohemia on the red, white and blue coat of arms of the Czech Republic.

Pedestrian crossing at the German Czech frontier near Zittau

Soon I emerged from the forest into the destitute Bohemian village of Hradek, which means little castle. Its poverty was in sharp contrast to the veneer of prosperity I had briefly become accustomed to in eastern Germany.

Curiously, I felt at home in Hradek, delighted at the sight of old Skoda cars, the smell of Czech sausages in the grocery store whose ancient scales bore the Cyrillic letters, "Made in USSR."

In front was a rusty bike rack and cement bench, spartan elements of life that I had come to enjoy in mid-1990s Prague. Most of all there was the lilting cadences of the Czech language.

The few people I encountered in Hradek were dark-skinned Romas or Gypsies, likely the children and grandchildren of people resettled here after 1945 when the Czechs expelled three million Germans from this area that was known as Sudetenland.

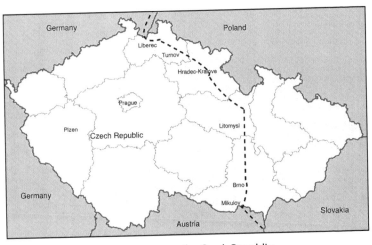

My route across the Czech Republic

Refreshed from the pit stop in Hradek, I contemplated the vexing question of *central* versus *eastern* Europe, a curious phenomenon that within this region has significance little appreciated elsewhere.

For example, if I am situated in Hradek 150 miles north of Prague, and thus considerably *west* of Vienna, how can I possibly be in Eastern Europe? Prior to the iron curtain and what might be called the convenient division of the continent into the rich democratic west and the poor communist east, Central or Middle Europe was a recognizable geographical term. In the pre-war period, Central Europe typically consisted of the German and Austrian lands, and what is now the Czech Republic, Poland, Slovakia, Hungary and a few other states.

While Central Europe can be a geographic entity, the region is diverse in language and culture, as seen in the differences between Germans and Slavs. Sudetenland, a crescent-shaped range of low mountains along the northern, western and southern borders of the Czech Republic, has been something of a natural demarcation line. But not surprisingly the border regions have been inhabited by both German and Slavic speakers.

While there's been considerable conflict between Czechs and Germans, in some ways they're quite similar. Both have a propensity to obey rules. Both value punctuality and precision. They share an affinity for sausages and dumplings. I agree with the adage that Czechs are the Prussians of the Slavic world.

Ruminating on geography and culture, I rode on, delighted that the mid-afternoon sky remained bright. My maps suggested that I could reach Liberec before nightfall. However, that was before I made a fateful detour onto what I thought was a shortcut.

Traveling east through a pleasant river valley, the hills grew steadily higher. At a crossroads called Bily Kostel, or white chapel, I came upon a signpost with a bicycle icon pointing off to the right. It indicated that the distance to Liberec via the bike trail was 15 miles, the same as on the highway. On a whim I turned onto the cycling trail, thinking it would be more interesting and free of traffic.

Unknown to me the trail ascended a 2,100-foot-tall mountain that the Czechs call Dlouha Hora or Long Mountain. That's a height greater than Lookout Mountain at Chattanooga.

Having started on this improbable course, as when I was lost in Poland, I resisted recurrent inclinations to turn back. Like a fool I blundered deeper into the forest and higher up the mountain. For three excruciating hours I plodded on, seeing not a single person. Steadily enveloped by forest, silence was broken only by the sounds of my bicycle tires and feet against fallen leaves and the crackling of brush when a deer bolted past in the distance. At times the trail was so steep that I had to push the bike. The pounding of my heart was so pronounced that I actually wondered if a beating heart was audible outside the body. It was pure misery.

On Long Mountain (Dlouha HoraDONE)

Finally I came to a signpost. Only then did I learn that I was atop Dlouha Hora, a mere 3 miles from where I had so foolishly diverted from the main road. The altitude was 700 meters, 2100 feet. What incredible stupidity. But of course I was glad to have reached the summit.

However, coming down in some ways was harder than going up. For much of the descent I was on a rutted logging trail littered with flat slippery stones, gullies, and fallen branches. My arms ached from being rigidly extended to the handlebars. At last I reached a paved road and soon arrived at Chrastava, back on the main road and only minutes away from where I so stupidly diverted onto the bike trail.

Exhausted, I finally arrived in Liberec where I was saddened to learn most hotels were filled for a convention. Finally I found a place. It was a communist-style high rise that not surprisingly had been passed over by the conventioneers. But I was in no position to be fussy and the people at the front desk were friendly. After placing the bicycle in a storage closet, the female clerk asked where I'd come from. I replied eastern Germany by way of Dlouha Hora. She answered, "no, I don't think you mean Dlouha Hora. That's a very tall mountain." Exhausted, all I could say was, "I know."

My room was illuminated by a single bulb that dangled at the end of a cord that hung from the ceiling. The television didn't work. Alas these were problems of no consequence. All I wanted was sleep.

In the morning I examined my maps. I had traveled 42 long, arduous miles from Ostritz.

Liberec is an interesting city that reflects the complicated history of North Bohemia. At the top of the main square is the grand, oversized Renaissance-style city hall that seems a carbon copy of Vienna's magnificent city hall. In fact it is a copy. The two edifices were designed by same architect.

Through most of its history and until the formation of Czechoslovakia in 1919, Liberec was German-speaking Reichenberg, which as part of Bohemia and Moravia was ruled from Vienna. For a hundred years Reichenberg was the textile center of the Austrian empire.

Following World War II the Czechs expelled the entire

Sudeten German population. Urban centers, including Reichen-berg with 30,000 Germans, were emptied out, often under brutal conditions.

Eager to get back on the road, I retrieved the bike from storage and was on my way headed south and east deeper into the Czech lands. There was heavy traffic but the real problem was a fierce headwind. In the first hour I traveled only eight miles. It took another hour to reach Turnov, a town only 16 miles from Liberec. Discouraged, I took a long break. Resuming the ride, my pace slowed even more to a mere seven miles per hour. When I reached Horice at 6:30 PM, where I stopped for the night, I had traveled 42 miles in seven and a half hours. My speed averaged a paltry 5.7 miles per hour.

I also experienced humiliation on the road to Horice. Late in the day—with the wind still strong—a young cyclist in racing kit, drew along beside me. He greeted me in Czech and then English. He said we could ride in tandem and he would practice his English. He said he was out for a quick 30-mile workout.

In a gesture he meant as helpful, my companion extended his right palm onto my lower back and essentially pushed. I felt humiliated but kept quiet. I imagined I was a stalled vehicle being towed to the garage. When his pushing didn't produce a faster speed, Jan, the 22-year-old cyclist, fumed, "you're carrying too much weight." Frustrated, he sped away saying he would wait for me at a bus station in the next town. I never saw him again.

North Bohemia, which I had now managed to cross, is a lot like my home state of Michigan. Its economy is a blend of industry and agriculture, lots of people in towns but few in the countryside. In Turnov I was within a few miles of the country retreat of former Czech president Vaclav Havel. Nestled amid green hills, Havel loved his secluded cottage. He did his best writing here in the country. During the time he was banished because of his anti-communist views, Havel had been a laborer in the Turnov brewery.

Vaclav Havel, the playwright president, died in 2011. To my mind he is the most significant leader to have emerged from post-communist Europe.

My next objective was Hradec Kralove, which without headwinds I might have reached the previous day. Back on the highway, I reached that pleasant industrial town in two hours. When I lived in Prague in the mid-1990s, I made several visits to Hradec Kralove because I was purchasing a Petrof grand piano from the factory that has been situated there for over a century and a half. I had also come to know the third and fourth generation Petrofs and written about their harrowing story of how the illustrious firm was nationalized by communists and then finally returned to the family in the 1990s. Coming out from the city, I rode past the factory and then past the Petrof home.

Czech Praga truck, produced from 1952 to 1989

Back in the countryside, I pedaled deeper into industrial Moravia, which together with Bohemia in Austrian times comprised the industrial heartland of the Hapsburg Empire. I passed Vysoke Myto and its big factory that manufactures Karosa buses.

Finally I came to Litomysl, birthplace of Bedrich Smetana, the early 19th century composer beloved by Czechs. Smetana composed the haunting tone poem *Ma Vlast* or "My Country," an unofficial national anthem. Litomysl is a wonderfully preserved medieval city that is attracting more and more tourists.

The next day at noon I traveled south over steep hills heading for the Moravian capital of Brno. Regrettably what began as a slow drizzle steadily worsened. Two hours into the ride I was soaked and stopped in a café to do a complete change of clothing and cover my luggage.

Amid light rain over the next hour I learned a lot about the importance of layering clothing. My outer windbreaker worked well in the cool weather but didn't permit perspiration generated from climbing to escape. Uncomfortable and cold, I found that by removing the windbreaker and shirt, and replacing them with a long sleeve shirt, a sweater and flannel vest, I was OK. Temperatures were in the 50s. I also found that when climbing, the beret I wore beneath my helmet dripped with sweat. If I removed it there was less perspiration. Conversely on downhill runs I wore the beret and my head wasn't chilled from the onrushing wind.

By late afternoon drizzle became downpour. After suffering for two additional hours I took shelter at Cerna Hora (Black Mountain) nine miles north of Brno. I was cold, drenched and miserable. Peering through dim light at a canopied bus stop, I dug out the last of my dry clothes and then again put on full rain gear. After waiting in vain for another 30 minutes, I gritted my teeth, turned on the rear light and rode slowly on.

At times the torrents of water from passing trucks hit me like waves crashing ashore and it was hard to retain balance. My midsection absorbed the steady rush of rain propelled upwards from the spinning front wheel, which had no fender. I continually wiped my face in order to see.

After a few more miles streetlights announced that I had

come to a village. Everything was closed except for a beer hall. I parked and went inside but the revelers merely stared at me. No one spoke English. At last the barkeep came over and I indicated with hand signs and rudimentary Czech that I needed a place to stay. He pointed to the east, apparently to another road that paralleled this highway a few miles north of Brno.

I ventured back into the downpour and rode along the residential street to which I had been directed. Some minutes later I came upon two strollers sheltering beneath a large umbrella. Soaked and desperate, I asked the young couple if there was a hotel nearby and they replied in English!

To my eternal gratitude, Tereza Bartos and her friend Robert immediately offered assistance. "Come with us," said Tereza, "our home is just ahead. We'll give you warm clothes and hot tea." They were the sweetest words I could imagine.

We arrived at their substantial single-family house. My bike and its soaked luggage were parked undercover and following the young couple I stepped into the foyer. Tereza's mother Helena was making dessert pancakes (palacinky) in the kitchen while her father Karel kept her company. The family seemed delighted to receive an unexpected, disheveled visitor from America. We were six miles from Brno, they said. While I dried off in the spare bedroom, I heard Tereza on the phone inquiring about accommodation. Soon we were seated at the dining room table eating palacinky and discussing the state of the world.

Tereza and Robert were graduate students at university. Robert was pursuing engineering, Tereza teacher training. Thirty minutes later Karel, Robert and I loaded the bike and wet gear into the family's Peugeot wagon. We said our farewells and the men drove me to the city and the hotel that had been booked.

This had been my worst day but with a happy ending. Settling into my room in the Hotel Akord, I used every inch of floor space spreading out my soaked belongings, hoping that some things would be partially dry by the next day.

After the rain, leaving Brno

In the morning the sun was out. I toured the city that in Austrian times was Brunn. It is the second largest city in the Czech Republic and near the border with Austria. Like Liberec, Brno had been cleared of its ethnic German population following World War II.

In Brno there is a memorial to the composer Leos Janacek who came from here. Nearby is the birthplace of another Czech composer, Gustav Mahler, whose life reflects the tribulations of multi-ethnic pre-war Europe. Born in 1860, Mahler was Jewish and grew up speaking German. In her biography of her husband, Alma Mahler suggests that the composer converted to her Catholicism in order to obtain the prestigious post of conductor of the Vienna State Opera. She wrote that Mahler often said, "I am thrice homeless, as a native of Bohemia in Austria, as an Austrian among Germans, and as a Jew throughout the world.

Everywhere an intruder, never welcomed."

Leaving from the Akord Hotel, the proprietor kindly ran off a map of the route to the border. I thanked him and rode off, curiously thinking not of Brno, but of Prague and the wonderful three years I had spent in the Czech capital.

I thought in particular of Mahler's statement of being thrice homeless. I remembered the response of a Czech friend when I referred to Franz Kafka as a great Czech writer. To my surprise the comment provoked the rejoinder, "Kafka wasn't Czech," said my friend, "he was German and Jewish and happened to live in Prague." I learned to keep my mouth shut about the complexities of Czech identity.

However, I learned more about multiculturalism from a remarkable American, Alan Levy, who from 1991 until his death in 2004 was editor-in-chief of the *Prague Post*, the leading English language weekly in post-communist Europe. Alan played a huge part in making Prague the magical in "place" for thousands of youthful expatriates in the 1990s. Levy spoke Czech and loved the city he had known since 1967 when he arrived from Vienna to write about the Prague Spring that briefly flourished under the reform communist Alexander Dubcek. Levy was in Prague when the Russians invaded in August 1968.

A Jewish New Yorker, Levy told me that in the decades leading up to the Second World War, the Sunday custom was for Prague's Czech majority to stroll along Narodni Trida, the boulevard that passes the National Theater, while the German speaking minority, mostly Jewish, took their constitutionals a few blocks away on na Prikope.

Levy wrote that his life changed when he was asked to edit the *Prague Post*.

*In the summer of 1991, two young Americans—Lisa Frankenberg and Kent Hawryluk, both born in the watershed year of 1968—approached me about founding*

> *an English-language weekly newspaper and, at age fifty-nine and a half and after thirty-one years of freelancing, I underwent the best midlife career change I know: moving to the other end of the desk as editor-in-chief of the Prague Post and writing a weekly "Prague Profile" column... It turned out to be the job for which I had been rehearsing all my life.*

The *Prague Post* gave voice to the hundreds of young Americans who lived in the city in the 1990s. In its first issue, in November 1991, Levy famously compared Prague to Paris in the '20s, calling the Czech capital an adventurous haven for aspiring writers:

> *We are living in the Left Bank of the '90s. For some of us, Prague is Second Chance City; for others a new frontier where anything goes, everything goes, and, often enough, nothing works. Yesterday is long gone, today is nebulous, and who knows about tomorrow, but, somewhere within each of us, we all know that we are living in a historic place at a historic time.*

Having lived in Prague during that magical time, I think Alan had it exactly right. Endlessly quoted by the media, Levy's words drew the young, Pied Piper-style, to the ancient, remarkably preserved Bohemian city.

I once asked Levy, why Prague, instead of Budapest or Berlin? How did that happen?

"I've thought a lot about that," he replied. "I think the answer is Vaclav Havel." There was, said Levy, something compelling about a modest literary person becoming president. Then, he grumbled on, "By rights it should have been Berlin." The formerly divided German capital, he said, had the infamous wall and had been first to be liberated. But Berlin didn't have Havel.

Neither did the other capitals have The Globe bookstore, a second icon of Prague's American period. It was started in

1993 by five young Americans who thought a new generation of expats needed a place to hang out, drink coffee, and browse. It began with hurried trips home to collect books to fill the shelves. The concept succeeded and comported with Levy's delicious Paris theme. The name, of course, is derived from Shakespeare and Company, the bookshop on the Left Bank popularized by Hemingway and his circle in the 1920s.

The Globe bookstore in the 1990s (Mark Baker photo)

The Globe worked, I think, because it was authentic. Prices were low and the time was right. Open until late, it served an American breakfast and all types of coffee. The Globe got the English language newspapers earlier than the competition and carried British and American magazines. The Globe's appeal was enhanced by it being situated in the unfashionable Holosevice district, far away from the tourist track. Ah yes, I thought, golden Prague, zlata Praha, at its zenith.

But it was now two in the afternoon on Monday and I was still in Brno and needing to reach Mikulov, 33 miles south next to the Austrian border.

I arrived in Mikulov at 7 and chose a small hotel with geraniums in its window boxes. Later walking through the town I was surprised by the parade of Austrian cars on the street. Austrians had come to shop because of the lower prices on the Czech side of the border.

I remembered that a friend in Washington told me that during communism ordinary Austrians would never think of crossing into Czechoslovakia. "All we knew," she said, "was that they were poor and couldn't travel. It never occurred to me that I would want to visit."

Taking stock of my travel, from Litomysl to Brno I had come 44 miles, not bad, I thought, considering the horrid weather. And now I had added another 33 miles from Brno to Mikulov.

The next day I started earlier and rode on to the place where the iron curtain had been. During communism there was always a wide swath of unpopulated territory adjacent to the border. This was still the case as I climbed a gentle hill and approached the frontier.

# V.

# AUSTRIA, SLOVAKIA, HUNGARY, AND SERBIA

At the Czech-Austrian border green vineyards fanned out in all directions. On the Austrian side the vines were meticulously groomed, on the Czech side less so. Weeds had sprouted, vines needed pruning. It was the same terrain and yet the quality gap between Austrian and Moravian whites began with the vines and continued through to the modern tanks and winemaking equipment visible on the Austrian side. During four decades of state ownership under communism the Czech wine industry was starved of needed investment.

During the three years I lived in Prague in the 1990s Czech wines were ridiculed while Austrians were highly regarded. Privatization and long overdue investment should close the gap.

I deliberately chose a route that cut through Austria to get some sense of lingering differences between east and west.

The decades in which living standards had been higher in Austria were immediately apparent. Villages were modern, roads, sidewalks, and public amenities were well maintained. People were better dressed, their homes were modern and often renovated, and of course the cars were newer. Grocery store prices were higher but incomes were also much higher. Everything seemed an improvement over what I had experienced during weeks of cycling in the east.

I rode in a southeasterly direction towards the Slovak capital of Bratislava over 35 miles of secondary roads and tranquil lanes in Austria that sloped east towards the Morava or River March that is the border between Austria and Slovakia. Country life seemed idyllic—cows grazing on hillsides, farm tractors occasionally clattering towards tidy villages. Behind me a sleek red commuter train zipped along, carrying travelers to Vienna, a 45-minute ride away.

After some time I reached Angern where a motorized barge carried cars and trucks across the Morava to Slovakia. Once across I arrived in the village of Zahorska Ves, which means "behind the mountain" in Slovak. It was my third country in half a day.

Ferry across the Morava River, Zahorska Ves

You can throw a ball across the narrow Morava at Angern. Words shouted on one side are easily heard on the other. And yet from 1948 until 1989 this gentle stream was a cold war barrier cruelly dividing east from west.

Riding into the village of Zohor, a short distance from the

river, the tableau appeared unchanged from what it must have been for decades. Stopping by the roadside, I watched an old woman in black wearing a babooshka and carrying a shopping bag walk slowly past. Two old men pedaled along very slowly on ancient bicycles. A woman leaned from a second story window to pour water on red geraniums in her flower boxes. Identical dwellings were flush to the sidewalk and marched in a neat row towards the graceful spire of the Catholic church a block away.

Beyond the church the dinging of a small bell and the lowering of a crossing gate announced the arrival of a burgundy and yellow single train car from Bratislava, 12 miles to the south. A tall man in a wide-brimmed hat carrying a suitcase got off and walked towards the village. The train car trundled off, leaving behind stillness broken only by the occasional cooing of doves. I rode past the local hospoda or beer garden where a few bikes and motorbikes leaned against the building. Through the open door came laughter and the smell of pilsner.

At 9 PM I arrived at the larger town of Stupova. Wanting to spend the night at my favorite hotel in Bratislava, I locked the bike to a pole, gathered my baggage and inquired at a pub about buses to the capital. There were none at this late hour, I was told, but a young man got up from a table and said in perfect English that he was headed into town and that I could ride with him.

His name was Ivan and he drove an old Peugeot 404. He had recently returned from a year of working in Ireland. He said he was making good money in Bratislava as a computer repairman. Dropping me at the hotel, he was gone.

In the morning I boarded a regional bus and returned to Stupova. I retrieved the bike, attached the panniers and pedaled south towards Devin, where the Morava empties into the wide, formidable Danube. It was a scenic route to the capital that took me along the perimeter of the unusual 1,500-foot Devinska Mountain that looms down over the junction of the two rivers. At Devin the road makes a sharp turn. Suddenly I was on the banks of the majestic—and not at all blue—Danube.

In the early 19th century the Austrian statesman Prince Metternich famously observed that, "East of Vienna the Orient begins." But here in Devin, amid the green hills that are only 35 miles downstream from Vienna, his assertion seemed ridiculous.

I parked the bike and sat in a chair carved from the stump of a tree at a trellised wine bar. I watched Danube towboats silently slide past bearing coal, coiled steel sheets and cars. The river was so wide that it was hard to make out the flags of the vessels that hugged the opposite shore. On one I finally made out the red, green and white tricolor of Hungary, on another the yellow and blue banner of Ukraine.

At the next table sat an Irishman and a Slovak who obviously had been drinking for some time. Cedric, who said he was a wine importer from Dublin, told the story of Slovak champagne with the brand name Hubert. "It was started by an officer in Napoleon's army," he said in his wonderful Irish brogue, "who deserted after the battle at Wagram just across the river. This man Hubert," he continued, "enjoyed his life here so much that he began to make champagne from the local grapes. It's all survived down to the present day." The champagne indeed exists, but as to Cedric's story, who knows.

Refreshed I mounted the bike, turned the corner and headed east to the Slovak capital.

I passed the huge Volkswagen plant that was a useful introduction to the industrial modernization that occurred in Slovakia after the collapse of communism. The VW factory occupies the equivalent of 21 football fields and employs 7,500 workers. It is a critical component in VW's global supply chain as components arrive daily by train from western Germany. Slovakia has four vehicle assembly plants and has become a Detroit of Eastern Europe.

I rode on towards the city. Patrick Leigh Fermor, arguably the greatest travel writer of the 20th century, trod this river trail in 1934 during his epic journey on foot across Europe. In *A Time of Gifts* Fermor described his approach to the Slovak capital:

> *The steep ascending city ... had been visible for miles. It was the old city of Pressburg, re-baptised with the Slav name of Bratislava when it became part of the new Czechoslovak Republic. The climbing hills were dominated by a hill and the symmetry of the huge gaunt castle and the height of its corner towers that gave it the look of an upside-down table.*

Bratislava Castle with its red tiled roof and conical turrets at the corners still resembles an upside-down table. Commanding the heights above the Danube, this ancient citadel had been a Hungarian fortification to halt the Turkish advance up the Danube. Having lost their capital Budapest to the Turks in 1526, the Hungarians or Magyars moved west to Bratislava, which they called Pozsony. The decisive Christian victory over the Turks at the gates of Vienna came later in 1683.

Bratislava Castle from the river's edge in the Slovak capital

For 250 years Hungarian monarchs were crowned in Pozsony's gothic St. Martin's Cathedral. Sadly the architectural unity of the castle, church and Jewish Quarter was obliterated by the communists' decision to wedge a freeway over the Danube between the church and the castle.

The Czechs and Slovaks, whose languages are mutually understandable, joined to become Czechoslovakia after the dissolution of the Austro Hungarian Empire. The new nation's independence lasted only until 1939 when Nazi Germany invaded the Czech lands and declared Slovakia a German protectorate. After the Second World War the communists ruled until the peaceful velvet revolution of November 1989.

With the restoration of freedom, Slovaks were restive, their national aspirations unfilled while judging themselves dominated by the more numerous, richer Czechs. Slovak independence, the velvet divorce, occurred in 1993. Since then Bratislava has blossomed from regional town into booming national capital. Both countries were among the former communist states that joined NATO and the European Union in 2004. Slovakia, however, one-upped the Czechs by joining the euro currency zone five years later.

Bratislava's prosperity is visible in its several glass and steel towers, renovations and streets crowded with shoppers. The small but charming old town winding uphill near the center is a welcome counterpoint to a still disfigured riverfront.

I cycled along the embankment and then joined a secondary road that meanders with the Danube east through low areas that comprise the best farmland in Slovakia.

With Bratislava only 50 miles from Vienna the two capitals are almost twin cities. Many travelers to Slovakia arrive at Vienna's airport where frequent shuttles take them to Bratislava. With Austria and Hungary close neighbors, it's not a surprise that the Slovak capital has had three names—Pozsony, Pressburg and Bratislava.

My route through Slovakia

After two hours of riding I arrived in Samorin, a town with a mixed Slovak and Hungarian population. I had traveled 34 miles.

The next morning amid a steady rain I rode on, leaving the Danube shore but never far from it. At Gabcikovo, adjacent to the lake made from a controversial dam, a heavy downpour forced me off the road for 90 minutes. When the rain subsided I rode on to Zemianska Olca and then Komarno, back on the Danube.

About this time I had the good fortune of meeting two other cyclists, a young married couple, Marek and Olga, who were out for a two-day ride and were now headed back to their home in Bratislava. Speaking in perfect English, Marek said he thought he knew me and amazingly he was correct! We had met in 1993 at what had been a communist party training center at Celakovice, a small town north of Prague. Marek was a student in the University of Pittsburgh MBA program that was based there and I was doing a week-long seminar for economics journalists. We had mutual friends.

Marek and Olga described Slovakia's break from Czechoslovakia in 1993 as a seminal event that cast off all kinds of demons, leading to their country's unsteady but ultimately successful transition from nationalist isolation to burgeoning prosperity. Independence, they agreed, did away with Slovaks' insular and defensive mentality borne from decades of perceived injustice. "Before independence," said Marek, "we could always blame the Czechs for our shortcomings. Now we've had to take responsibility for ourselves."

This harsh but positive assessment echoed a critique I had heard earlier from Irish-born Vincent Boland, who was the *Financial Times* correspondent in Central Europe. During a train ride from Bratislava to Prague, Vincent explained his strong affinity for the Slovaks. "They're so much like us [meaning the Irish]," he said. "Slovakia is really a post-colonial country with the same negative traits of self-centeredness, and of being narrow and nationalist."

Delighted with this chance meeting and dissection of the Slovak psyche, I rode on and soon came to Komarno, a large and complicated Slovak town on the Danube.

I quickly learned that Komarno is essentially a Hungarian place inside Slovakia. The predominant language is Hungarian. Hearing Hungarian—so different from Slavic languages—I was reminded that prior to the First World War all of Slovakia was ruled by Hungary.

In Komarno's cobblestoned town square stands an imposing statue of a Hungarian, General Gyorgy Klapka, hero of the failed 1848 Hungarian revolt against the Austrians. Sword drawn, cloak trailing from his shoulders, Klapka is unmistakably Hungarian. That this statue has been in place for over 100 years, for me, is evidence that despite recurrent inter-ethnic tension, tolerance and respect for shared history prevails.

Strolling the city's waterfront surveying the tall cranes of the shipyard that was Komarno's biggest employer, I was reminded that Hungary was the big loser in the First World War. In creating the new states of Czechoslovakia and Yugoslavia and greatly expanding the size of Romania, Woodrow Wilson and the peacemakers at Versailles took away two-thirds of Hungary's territory, leaving a third of Hungarians living outside their country. The border changes, codified in the 1920 Treaty of Trianon, are illustrated below.

My route through Hungary, Serbia and western Romania

The next morning I took a final glance at Komarno's town square and as muffled church bells chimed eight o'clock I crossed the Danube River bridge into Hungary, one of my favorite Central European countries.

I was now in Komarom, the southern part of a once undivided Hungarian city. Examining my maps I was equidistant from Budapest and Bratislava, each 60 miles away.

I had entered the broad plains of Magyarorszag, the Hungarian name for their country. Riding south into the countryside I could faintly see on the eastern horizon the green Esztergom hills closer to Budapest. There was little traffic and I was left to contemplate the serenity of abundant cornfields nearing harvest.

On my first visit to post-communist Hungary in March 1991, I asked Gabor Benczik, who then headed the journalists' association, how things were going. Seated in his spare, book-lined office on Budapest's main avenue, I was puzzled by the young man's cryptic reply: "It's as if all of our unresolved problems were put into the refrigerator when the communists took over in 1945. Now 46 years later, we've opened the fridge and discovered that the problems are still fresh, just as we left them."

I asked Gabor what he meant. Surely, I said, the future must be bright with communism over and the people having choices and freedoms they had only dreamed of. Speaking with the seriousness and irony that is characteristic of Hungarians, Gabor explained that he was referring to big questions like who should own Hungary's main assets—the land and factories—that were still under government control. After decades of suppressing ethnic identities, he wondered what it meant to be Hungarian. How should an independent Hungary relate to neighboring countries that had significant Hungarian minorities? And what about those minorities, he continued? They considered themselves Hungarian, spoke Hungarian, and yet were living in foreign and sometimes hostile lands.

Make no mistake, Hungarians are different from the Slavs who inhabit the neighboring territories. Some of the differences are distinct, such as the Slavic "good morning," which in Serbian is "dobro yutro," and Czech, "dobre rano." By contrast in Hungarian it's "jo napot." Hungarians always refer to one another with surnames first, as in Liszt Ferenc, not Franz Liszt. In addition Hungarians are often not well regarded by their Slavic neighbors. That is a legacy of history, a belief that the mere presence of this alien Magyar tribe in Central Europe stymied Slavic unity. Hungarians similarly lose points for their partnership with imperial Austria.

Riding on I crossed the Vienna-Budapest freeway and then followed the north-south road that threaded between hills on either side. By late afternoon I had come 44 miles and reached the prosperous city with the unpronounceable name—Sfekesfehervar—situated near Lake Balaton, a 50-mile-long, slender body of water that is Hungary's principal summer resort. Sfekesfehervar sparkled. Its name means "seat of the white castle."

Having made my way through the city to its southern outskirts, I stopped at an ATM to get Hungarian forints and approached a young couple sipping wine from stemmed glasses at an outdoor café. I asked whether I would find accommodation if I pressed on to the south. After talking among themselves, they said if I went another ten miles or so, I would find a castle that had been recently been made into a hotel. It was big, they said, and since it wasn't well known to travelers, it might offer cheap accommodation.

My bike at the entrance to Seregelyes Palace

They counseled me to watch for signs reading "kastely," castle in Hungarian. As darkness was some hours away, I took their advice and rode on. Eventually I came to the sign, turned east, passed through woods and then came upon a vast estate enclosed by a tall fence. I rang a bell, a security gate swung open, and I rode my Cannondale along a crushed gravel drive where I imagined the carriages of central European nobility once rolled. I arrived at a vast pastel-colored, 19th century manor house whose classical architecture was a grander version of George Washington's Mount Vernon. I was reminded of Jelgava Castle back in Latvia.

Directed to an office at the far end of the building, it was apparent that there were no other guests. The young woman at the desk was mildly surprised by my arrival but replied that there was a vacancy, priced beyond my budget but a bargain considering where I was. I took the room for the equivalent of $95, an amount then equal to more than a week's wage for an unskilled Hungarian. Collecting my belongings, I ascended the main staircase, found my room and laid the dusty panniers on the polished hardwood floors of a magnificent high-ceilinged chamber with a gigantic bed and tall window that looked out over 54 acres of manicured gardens and forests.

Informed that the restaurant was closed, I got back on the bicycle and rode off to a restaurant a mile and a half away. Over pizza and beer, which the Hungarians call "sor," (pronounced "sure" as in "sure thing"), I calculated that I had been on the road for 8½ hours and ridden 54 miles from Komarno.

I learned later that Seregelyes Palace dates from 1824. It was built by a Hungarian aristocrat who was loyal to the Hapsburgs in Vienna. A century later the estate was owned by another count whose daughter was the wife of Hungary's ambassador to the United States. Alas, during and after the Second World War the castle was ransacked, its priceless heirlooms looted.

Amazingly, feudalism essentially persisted in Hungary under the dual monarchy with Austria until the First World War. Estates like this were numerous as landed gentry—a mere few dozen families—controlled the government and economy. As late as 1940 one percent of the population owned half of Hungary's arable land.

On his trek from Holland to Turkey in 1934, Patrick Leigh Fermor recounted in *A Time of Gifts* a visit to a Hungarian estate not far away, where he enjoyed the hospitality of a baron for an entire week. Fermor's description might have applied to Seregelyes:

> *The house had the charm of a large and rambling rectory occupied by a long line of bookish and well-to-do incumbents torn between rival passions for field sports and their libraries... the library was so crammed that most of the paneling was hidden and the books, in German and French and English, had overflowed in neat piles on the floor. The surviving area of wall was filled by antlers and roebuck horns, a couple of portraits and a Rembrandt etching.*

In the morning, the full glory of Seregelyes was on display. I drew open lace curtains, pulled back shutters over casement windows and gazed onto a courtyard bathed in sunlight, a chestnut tree in the center. Later, crunching along gravel footpaths, I was transported back in time, as if Mozart or Haydn in powdered wigs and frock coats would come around the corner.

At the front desk there was another reality. The pleasant receptionist—a young woman of 29—told me that economically her life had been better ten years earlier. Here in central Hungary the average monthly wage was little more than $300.

There is in Hungary a widening gap between rich and poor, a phenomenon that was not nearly as glaring during communism. Perceived injustice at the hands of others as well as national failure was something people often spoke of.

Reluctantly departing from the luxury of Seregelyes, I cycled on through central Hungary following the Danube, which flowed south from Budapest as it made its way to Serbia. The countryside was golden with sunflowers and corn but people were poor and horse carts as common as tractors. At 4 PM I came to Dunafoldvar, which means "fortification on the Danube."

Two-horse wagon in a village near Dunafoldvar, Hungary

The town is 60 miles downstream from Budapest. Approaching the bridge I spotted a sleek white vessel with two rows of windows headed upstream. Hurrying onto the old steel bridge, I watched the elegant tour boat *Mozart* from Passau, Germany slide silently by. Some passengers were seated in the dining room looking out through sealed windows. Others were on deck to view Dunafoldvar. I guessed that the *Mozart* would have set out from Belgrade that morning. The luxury craft gone, I pedaled slowly into wooded sparsely populated countryside.

Turning my back on the Danube for a second time, I found myself thinking about the great river. What an incredible body of water. Returning to the Danube after two days away from it, I contemplated both its beauty and tortuous history. Before modern roads and the automobile the Danube was a highway that connected disparate cultures from southern Germany to the Black Sea.

Italian author Claudio Magris wrote in his 1989 book, *Danube,* that the river "threads towns together like a string of pearls." He argues that it is in Hungary where the Danube is

A tourist boat on the Danube at Dunafoldvar

most vital. It bisects the capital, Buda and Pest, and has been a conduit for war and conquest.

In the 15th and 16th centuries the Ottoman Turks worked their way up the Danube, taking Belgrade, then Budapest, until their penetration of the European main was halted at Vienna in 1683.

Here in southern Hungary, at Mohacs on the Danube, the Turks in 1526 defeated a Christian army of Hungarians, Bohemians and Austrians. It was, says Magris, the greatest catastrophe in Hungarian history, opening the way to 200 years of Turkish occupation that forced the Magyars to move their capital to Bratislava. He argues that the Mohacs disaster is central to Hungarian identity. Haunted by the loss to the Turks, Magris writes, Hungarians ask, "Are we always going to be defeated?"

I rode on and at 7 PM I reached Kiskoros, a medium-sized town in the southern wine district. I had come 50 miles and was delighted that in just two days I had very nearly crossed

Hungary from north to south. Geographically I was directly south of Budapest and midway between the capital and the Serbian border.

I found a hotel and while still in the lobby I was regaled by a British visitor about the rich business opportunities in the region. "You should buy vineyards," he said, "because prices are low and Hungarians are selling."

His message was that times were tough and unlikely to get better. He was pessimistic about Hungary. After the Wall came down, he said, IBM came to Hungary because workers were skilled and wages low. But after a few years IBM left and moved its computer-related Hungarian manufacturing to China.

Marta Kecskemeti in Kiskoros

As I prepared to depart in the morning I met Marta Kecskemeti at the tourist office. She was 27, recently married, and had been an exchange student in North Carolina where she mastered the English language. She had only recently returned to Kiskoros after seversal years in Budapest. We spent a leisurely hour talking about Hungary and its future. Marta's relative pessimism surprised me. She was convinced that in this part of

Hungary many people are worse off economically than they had been under communism.

Leaving Kiskoros at midmorning, I hoped to be in Serbia by nightfall. As I rode south there was evidence of economic distress. "Elado" (For Sale) signs were posted in fields and on cars parked in front of homes.

I departed Hungary sobered but with a sense that things would eventually come right. Not one person I met wanted a return to the old days. Rather, they wanted good government and rapid economic growth. They wanted better wages so that they could travel.

With its zesty food, strong wine, and strikingly different language, Hungary stands out. After centuries of foreign domination, the Magyars like the other nations forced to live under communism are free and reconnected to the west. Like their neighbors they see prospects for a better life but for most Hungarians that goal remains elusive.

\* \* \*

Reaching the border post at Tompa at mid-afternoon, I crossed into Serbia. Poor as rural Hungary was, Serbia was poorer. It was as if I had fallen off an economic cliff. I cycled past boarded up duty free shops on the Serbian side that must have done a brisk business when Hungarians came to buy consumer goods that were cheaper or unavailable at home.

Signs of poverty were everywhere. At the border, cars were lined up heading to Hungary but few went the other direction. Riding on, the centerlines on the road needed paint, corn in the fields was stunted for want of fertilizer, houses needed repair.

Geographically the land had not changed. It was flat, agriculturally abundant, part of the vast Pannonian plain of old Hungary. Northern Serbia is called Vojvodina and was part of Hungary until 1920. Subotica (Szabatka in Hungarian), six miles from the border, is the center of the remaining Hungarian presence in Vojvodina, the most ethnically diverse part of Serbia. Albert Einstein was a frequent visitor as his first wife came from a prosperous Vojvodina family.

At 6 PM I was in the center of Subotica. It had been a comfortable 42-mile ride from Kiskoros. Checking into the communist-era Patria Hotel, I got a sense of local sensitivities when the women at the front desk were insulted when I asked if they were ethnic Hungarians. "No," they replied indignantly, "we are proud Serbs."

About a third of Subotica's 100,000 inhabitants are ethnic Hungarian. Strolling through the town center, it was apparent that the city's finest buildings date back to the Hungarian period. Among them is the large Jewish synagogue and the magnificent art deco city hall, a towering, arcaded structure from 1906 with a decorative pitched roof and distinctive brick and stucco exterior.

What I liked best about Subotica was the effusiveness and energy I felt on city streets. People were demonstrative and outgoing. Laughter resonated from outdoor cafes and the streets were crowded. This was a big change from dour, often sullen Hungary.

In the morning I raised the nationality question with young ethnic Hungarians and got reassuring responses. Acquaintances in Hungary, learning that I was headed to Serbia, invariably expressed worry about their 200,000 brethren there. There had been well-publicized incidents of anti-Hungarian violence.

Ethnic Hungarian Robert Kovacs, 27, worked in the city tourist office. He dismissed the anti-Magyar enmity saying it had been orchestrated by corrupt Milosevic-era Serbian politicians trying to curry favor with the 200,000 or so Serbs who were resettled in Vojvodina after they were driven out of Croatia and Bosnia in the mid-1990s. These relative newcomers, said Robert, lacked the tradition of tolerance that characterized Vojvodina. He and other ethnic Hungarians I met said they had not felt the sting of ethnic discrimination.

Robert Kovacs, Hungarian language banner and Subotica town hall behind

\* \* \*

Disillusioned revolutionist Robertino Knjur at a café in Subotica

I sought out an acquaintance from the anti-Milosevic demonstrations in Belgrade that I had covered some years earlier. Robertino Knjur, a leader of the student revolt that in 2000 toppled Slobodan Milosevic, told me he was disgusted with politics and had dropped out of political protest. Now a teacher of mathematics, Knjur was cynical. "All our politicians are hopelessly corrupt," he said. He continued, instead of politics, "I spend my free time sailing on the Tisza River," not far from Subotica.

I departed Subotica riding east towards the Tisza River and Romania. The south-flowing Tisza—a formidable river—is a major tributary of the Danube.

Hungary's dominion over this part of Serbia—Vojvodina— extended north from Zemun, a cross-river western suburb of Belgrade that is 70 miles south of Subotica.

Belgrade, which means the white city, is situated where the River Sava joins the Danube. Here on the bluff above the confluence of the rivers the Turks built their principal river fort, Kalemegdan. Even today it is the defining geographic element of the Serbian capital.

At Kalemegdan, wrote the English writer Rebecca West in the 1930s, the Balkans begin. She likened Kalemegdan to a ship, whose "prow juts out between two great rivers and looks eastward over the great Pannonian Plain that spreads across Hungary towards Central Europe."

In 1915 American war correspondent Jack Reed crouched behind Serbian military lines at Kalemegdan, looking "at the muddy Danube and the wide plains of Hungary," witnessing Belgrade being pulverized by Austro-Hungarian artillery.

I set out from Subotica relying on regional maps. The map mounted atop my handlebar bag was so detailed that I had to change the fold every few miles. But I soon became aware of its inaccuracies.

I rode past lake resorts at Palic and came to the ethnic-Hungarian town of Kanjiza on the Tisza where Hungarian and

Serbian flags flew from the town hall. I then proceeded southeast past Mokrin near the Romanian border into the farming center of Kikinda. The land was rich, abundant with corn and sunflowers but sparsely populated. I went two miles once without seeing a person or physical structure. Six hours after departing Subotica, I arrived in Kikinda, having covered 50 miles.

Not knowing it, at Kikinda I was only miles from Lazarevo, the Vojvodina village that was the hiding place of Ratko Mladic, the alleged mastermind of the 1995 massacre at Srebrenica in Bosnia. Sixteen years on the run as Europe's most wanted man, Mladic was apprehended in May 2011.

A rail line dating back to Hungarian times connects Kikinda to the Romanian town of Jimbolia ten miles away. My map indicated that the trail I was following east from Kikinda was actually a road. In fact it was only a rutted path for farm vehicles. The map also indicated that the border crossing was for Serbian and Romanian passport holders only.

Amid cornfields on an apparent path to nowhere, I asked one of the few farmers that I encountered what to do. Trying to be helpful, he said my route wouldn't work and that I needed to cross at the larger frontier post, an 18-mile detour to the south.

Stubbornly I ignored his counsel. But two miles farther on, with the path petering out, a farmer in a battered Yugo was adamant. Leaving his car running, its door open, the burley fellow walked over, grabbed my map, studied it for a moment, and pointing emphatically with his meaty hand toward a man on a bicycle in the distance, said in German, "Fahren mit ihm!" Follow him. Thanking him, I sheepishly fell in behind the slow-moving cyclist and began the long ride back to the road I had sought to avoid. As I rode, I thought how stupid I had been and told myself to avoid being overconfident.

Two hours later I entered Romania through the lonely border crossing at Srpska Crnja.

My route through Romania to Calafat

# VI.

# ROMANIA

The Romania I entered at its western border was like northern Serbia—flat, boring and hot—providing no hint of great adventures ahead.

The remote border crossing near Jimbolia, which I had located only with difficulty, was forlorn. I was the only traveler.

As I rode off I heeded warnings from Serbian friends to be on guard for brigands who might spring from the bushes. Fearful of what I might be getting into, I lifted the bike's strong U lock from its holder and placed it into the handlebar bag in case it was needed for self defense.

I pedaled cautiously but there was no problem and indeed no people. I realized that the Serbs were repeating old stories from communism when Yugoslavs were freer and relatively rich while Romanians were destitute.

Surveying the stunted cornfields on either side I was unmistakably still in the flat embrace of the Banat, the great Hungarian plain that the Serbs call Vojvodina.

A single rail track paralleled the road and ran absolutely straight. The railroad had been built by Hungary when it controlled this vast fertile region.

I rode about 40 miles in strong but not searing heat. Closer to Timisoara I saw what looked like a statue at the side of the road. In fact it was an obelisk perched awkwardly between a cornfield and the road. Stopping, there was a recently constructed sign in multiple languages that declared that the European Union had rehabilitated the highway.

But there was more. While the stone obelisk had been patched, you could clearly see the inscription from 1835 that commemorated the completion of the road upon which I was traveling. It read:

> This road "faces the cold winter winds, the grey autumn's leaden rains, and the devastating scorching heat of the Banat."

Reflecting the multi-ethnic character of the Austro-Hungarian Empire, on the four sides of the obelisk near the base were explanatory words in Hungarian, German, Romanian and, amazingly, Latin. The distressing element was that the Hungarian language inscription had been defaced. It was my introduction to Romanians' lingering hostility towards Hungarians.

Riding on to Timisoara, its tall buildings rose up on the horizon. I was eager to get back to Timisoara, my favorite Romanian city that I first visited in 1994.

Timi, as locals call it, is agreeable, big but manageable and without the chaos of the capital Bucharest hundreds of miles to the east. Until coming under Romanian rule in 1920 Temesvar, its Hungarian name, was the second largest city in Hungary and its easternmost manufacturing center. Temesvar prided itself on being the first European city with electric streetlights.

Delighted to be back, I pushed the loaded bike through the downtown, past a busy McDonald's and trendy outdoor cafes that had sprouted since my last visit to a still shabby post-communist place. Reaching the tall Continental Hotel at the edge of downtown, I was eager to see if my friend Adrian Maran was still there. Adi was the first person I had met in Timisoara. Dressed in a burgundy jacket with epaulets, Adi was the hotel porter. He had greeted me in perfect English when I stepped down from the airport bus across the street from the hotel.

Locking the bike, I went into the lobby and to my delight Adi was behind the check-in counter. He had been promoted to front desk manager. Both of us were delighted to reconnect.

That evening Adi and I met for dinner and he filled me in on all that had happened since we last met. He and his Canadian girlfriend had just returned from a vacation in Italy. Adi said that while things had improved in Romania, corruption in politics and business remained huge problems.

Taking the next day off from riding, the next morning was Sunday and I went off in search of the church where the Romanian revolution began. Implausibly, the revolution had been launched at a Protestant church whose parishioners were ethnic Hungarians.

Of all the anti-communist revolutions in Europe, Romania's was bloodiest.

In the autumn of 1989 Pastor Laszlo Tokes was well known as a dissident and advocate for Timisoara's Hungarian minority. In November he was placed under house arrest and ordered into internal exile. His parishioners objected and barricaded the church to prevent his removal. With all of Eastern Europe in turmoil, Romanian students joined the protest, which quickly morphed into demands that President Nicholai Ceausescu resign. There were chaotic scenes and the Securitate secret police opened fire. Dozens were killed or wounded. The protests spread to the capital. Ceausescu and his wife fled but were caught near Timisoara and summarily executed.

Searching for the Biserica Reformata church, I was surprised that young people I approached for directions didn't have a clue. Finally, on the south bank of the River Tega near the downtown, I found it. But it wasn't a church at all. It was an early 20th century apartment block, whose second floor had been converted to a sanctuary. Hearing singing, I ascended the stairs and slipped into an empty pew as the Hungarian language service went on. There were only a few worshippers and most were elderly.

After the service the young pastor who was in charge told me that ethnic Hungarians remained under pressure, were discriminated against in terms of employment, and that young Hungarians were moving to Budapest. He said only 25,000 ethnic Hungarians remained in Timisoara.

The only hint that this nondescript place was central to the Romanian revolution was a small plaque on the building's exterior. Its inscription—*Here on December 15th, 1989, began the revolution that put an end to dictatorship*—was written in Hungarian and German.

Riding out from Timisoara the next day I was unsettled by the subtle but unmistakable anti-Hungarian sentiment I had observed.

At Adi's suggestion I set out for Lugoj 35 miles to the east on a secondary road that paralleled the main highway. As the sprawl of Timisoara receded, I relished being back in the relaxed embrace of country life. The rolling terrain and dense forest were unexpected treats.

Two hours from Timi a tapering church steeple rose up straight ahead. It was different from the helmeted Austrian style churches I'd observed since Poland, through the Czech and Slovak lands, Hungary and even Serbia. This one was a majestic conical spire that rose from the base of a rectangular bell tower. It was similar to the country churches I'd grown up with in Michigan.

Entering the village of Bakova it was apparent that the church was the only substantial building in the town. There was nothing else—not a stoplight or stop sign, only a row of modest houses on either side of the road. Bakova was so insignificant that it wasn't included on my Romanian map.

I paused in front of the church next to a small monument protected by a wrought iron fence. It was an 1868 German language marker that listed the dozen or so parishioners responsible for the church's construction. The building itself was in relatively good shape except for a few holes high up in the side windows. I hadn't expected to find a German church in this part of Romania.

As I stood at the front door, a battered Romanian Dacia sedan pulled up. A big shirtless man got out and I was momentarily afraid that this meant trouble. He walked briskly towards me, but then disarmingly asked in German if I would like to go inside. I was relieved and delighted. The man was Nikolaus Luncan, who would tell me he was the last German in Bakova.

Nikolaus Luncan at Bakova church

After we exchanged pleasantries, Nikolaus said that as recently as 1990 there had been 2,000 ethnic Germans in this area, but that after Ceausescu's demise they all gradually seized their new freedoms and moved to Germany. They had been farmers, he said, and spoke Romanian as well as German. They were Swabians from near the Rhine who in the late 18th century had been brought to this remote territory by Empress Maria Theresa. In all an estimated 100,000 Swabians were recruited to settle in Romania.

Nikolaus took from his pocket a slender metal key that unlocked the heavy wooden door of the church. Entering, we

gazed at the stained glass window behind the altar that was illuminated by the setting sun. I examined the old German language hymnals still neatly arrayed on the backs of the polished
wooden pews. Everything seemed to have been left as it was.
Nikolaus said there had been some problems, particularly when
rowdies had hurled stones that broke windows.

It was a magnificent country church. The pipe organ,
Nikolaus said, was built in Austria in the 1880s. His wife, he
said, occasionally came to play.

Looking at the empty pews, I wondered about the people
who used to fill them. How sad that they departed just as 44
years of communist dictatorship ended. As we said good-bye,
Nikolaus pointed down the road and said the next village, Buzias,
was renowned for its mineral water and that I should look for it.

The Swabian Germans endured a century of turmoil. In the
19th century the Hungarians promoted their language and culture at the expense of German. When the Austro-Hungarian
empire was dissolved in 1919 the Swabians awkwardly found
themselves inside independent Romania. During the later Nazi
period a German-language army division was raised in the
Banat. Hundreds never returned from the eastern front.

After the war the Romanian communists took revenge. By
the 1970s the remaining Swabians were destitute. The West
German government paid ransom money to get them out, but so
few exit permits were issued that only a trickle could leave. This
misery is the backdrop for the bleak writings of Herta Muller,
the 2009 Nobel Laureate, who grew up five miles from Bakova
and who herself migrated to Germany in the 1970s.

Shaken by the knowledge that terrible things had happened
in this beautiful land, I rode on towards Lugoj, hurrying as the
sun began to set. I was in woodlands now and tall trees dimmed
the remaining light. The air was fresh with layers of dampness
and chill invisibly rising from the pavement. I felt alone but
energized in a distant land.

About this time the handlebar bag laden with too many water bottles slipped from its clamp. A front pannier broke loose and bounced on the roadway. I stopped, tarrying for ten minutes of repairs and reflection. Looking around me there wasn't a sound. In a strange way I felt exhilaration. This journey, the farther east I ventured, had become a deeper adventure. Banat Romania was mysterious and mildly dangerous but also compelling and incredibly interesting.

It was dark when I arrived in Lugoj, whose western edge was grimy and poor with cobblestones that made riding difficult. Lugoj is a junction for the railway and the highway that veer south to the Danube through a Carpathian mountain pass. A less traveled road continues east into Transylvania. For some minutes I bumped along the back streets of Lugoj, past barking dogs and dimly lit homes searching for the thoroughfare where the big trucks to and from Turkey rumbled through.

Adi in Timisoara suggested that I stay at the Hotel Dacia. Coming upon it, from the outside it was uninviting. Situated on the main street, its entrance was dark. My expectations were low.

But there were pleasant surprises within. From behind a desk a middle-aged Romanian greeted me in German and said he was part of the Swabian community. He assigned me an upstairs room and pointed to the restaurant across the hall that was still open. Opening its door, I observed several diners seated at tables with starched tablecloths and cloth napkins.

Upstairs my well-appointed room harkened back to another time. The ceiling was high. There was an open transom above the door. Dark wainscot paneling extended halfway up the walls and then red wallpaper climbed to the ceiling. A tall interior shutter covered the casement window. I felt like a time traveler in a room similar to what I had heard my grandfather describe when he traveled North America as a tobacco salesman in the early 1900s.

Refreshing myself and putting on clean clothes, I descended

the staircase to the dining room where I found a handsome menu printed in Romanian and German. Framed etchings and old photographs were displayed on the walls. When the food arrived it was expertly presented. This unexpected panache and old world charm in what I thought would be a communist relic turned around my negative first impressions of Lugoj.

Midway through the meal a Greek highway engineer at the next table asked that I join him. Between swigs of beer and bites of filet of beef, he complained that in 24 months of supervising a European Union aid project, the Romanians had been able to complete only 30 miles of highway. "They're inept," he said, "and they will work only between April and September." As he continued his rant, my eye wandered to a table along the wall where two young women sat across from two middle-aged men. Throughout their meal no words were exchanged across the table as the men and the women conversed only with themselves. This appeared to be a business transaction.

The next morning at breakfast I met Helga Wingert, a physicist originally from Lugoj who had moved to Baden-Baden, Germany in 1978. She said she had grown up in a nearby village and went to school in Lugoj. This was her first return to Romania.

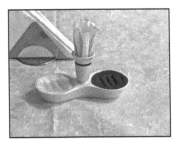

Salt and pepper

Curiously, our conversation began with my prosaic question about the old-fashioned salt and pepper service on the table. It was a ceramic dish with shallow bowls on either side of a tooth-pick holder. Helga demonstrated its use by delicately sliding the blade of a knife into the salt and then tapping with a fore-finger to spread the salt over her plate. Amused by my interest, Helga said the custom probably dated back to the Hapsburgs. How bizarre, I thought, that such an aristocratic practice had somehow survived the ravages of Romania's cruel, destructive brand of communism.

Despite professing to feeling out of place in the city where she once lived, Helga welcomed my coming along to her old school. We strolled pleasant side streets and then arrived at a three-story building with a fresh coat of yellow paint. This had been her high school. We pushed open the heavy wooden door and went inside. We were met by a janitor, an older man who at once remembered Helga. They chatted amicably in Romanian. Along the wall were portraits of the school's principals. She pointed to the dour visage of the man who ran the school during her time. "It's strange," said Helga, "during the Ceausescu regime standards in math and science remained quite high."

Outside, Helga told me how depressing it was to be back. She said she would not return again. She was glad she went to Germany early on and was not surprised that the rest of the Banat Germans followed as soon as they could. "We won't come back," she said, "even if we're asked." Shaking hands, we parted.

When I returned to the Dacia Hotel, one of the men who had been at the table with the two women the previous night approached me and asked in English if we hadn't seen one another at the Continental Hotel in Timisoara. I told him I had stopped there and that I remembered him. His name was Marco, from Milan. He said he came to Romania for the women. "It is paradise here," he said, "for a night with an attractive woman I pay only 10% of what I would pay at home." He said he was on a two-week Romanian vacation.

Shepherds with their flock near Lugoj

Departing Lugoj, the day was fresh and bright and I was heading south towards the mighty Danube. My pace had slowed but so what. In these Banat days I had been the recipient of rare gifts. The wonderful people I met extended not only hospitality but insight into local culture. I thought of this on the outskirts of Lugoj when I stopped for some minutes while shepherds directed their flock along the highway. Taking it in, I realized I was witnessing something seldom seen by outsiders.

I was now in the Cerna Valley. Riding on I recorded my progress. It was one hour to the village of Jena, 40 minutes more to Delcoveicu, another hour to Caransebes, and three miles to the village of Buchin where a young boy pointed with pride to the colorful tiles of traditional design that adorned the family home.

From Mehadia in the Cerna Valley it was 15 miles to the River Danube. Here I saw the most stunning landscapes I had yet experienced. The road and railway snake through this narrow valley where Carpathian peaks rise majestically on either side. More than once I steered to the shoulder to admire the tableau.

Traditional decorative tiles, Cerna Valley

The riding went well. For several miles I didn't see a tractor but instead men and women working the fields, cutting hay with scythes and raking with handcrafted wooden tools.

I passed farm wagons with hay piled perilously high. The metal wagon wheels grated against the pavement, an almost musical counterpoint to the rhythmic clomping of horses' hooves. Occasionally there would be the crack of a whip or a vocal command from the driver.

On his remarkable trek across Europe in 1934, Paddy Fermor must have trod this very road and observed the same labor-intensive agriculture. He wrote of passing a hillside, "...where a string of reapers were getting in the late upland harvest." He described "white-clad countrymen and women in wide hats of plaited straw." Little, it seems, had changed.

Pedaling on I knew this valley was once a path of empire. Trajan's legions came this way campaigning against the fierce Dacians, today's Romanians. Rome's annexation of Dacia in 106 A.D. was the empire's deepest penetration into the Balkans.

Advancing north they came upon the thermal springs they christened Baths of Hercules, today's Baile Herculane, only two miles east from the roadway. Franz Joseph, the Austrian emperor, had been a repeat visitor. He boasted in 1847, "we have, in the Valley of Cerna, the most beautiful spa on the continent."

Haying

Plowing

In early evening I reached the Danube, which spread out before me like a lake. I was stunned at its breadth.

In his book *Between the Woods and the Water*, Paddy Fermor had similarly emerged from the forest:

> ... *all at once the sides of the valley fell away and revealed the towers and trees of Orsova, then the troubled and blue-grey waters of the Danube and the palisade of the Serbian mountains beyond.*

Exhausted from six hours and 42 miles in a bike saddle, I rode the short distance into Orsova and registered at the communist-like Hotel Flora where I was the only guest. When I inquired about a restaurant, the manager switched on the lights in the dining room and kitchen and made me an omelet.

At Orsova I had reached what Fermor called, "the end of middle Europe." That was an accurate description as late as 1920 when Orsova was the farthest-most penetration of Hapsburg lands. Here Mitteleuropa ended and terra incognita began.

Despite the area's history reaching back 2,000 years, few travelers know about the Iron Gate region. And here I differ with Fermor. When he returned to Orsova in the 1970s, he wrote that the communist era Iron Gate Dam had raised the Danube 150 feet, emasculating the region's beauty and charm:

> *This has turned a hundred and thirty miles of the Danube into a vast pond which has swollen and blurred the course of the river beyond recognition. It has abolished canyons, turned beetling crags into mild hills and ascended the beautiful Cerna valley almost to the Baths of Hercules.*

While it is true that the landscape was inexorably altered and that the Orsova Fermor knew is gone, submerged in the lake that was created behind the dam, beauty remains. Old Orsova was no doubt far more appealing than the newer communist town that retained its name. Equally tragic is the loss of Adeh Kaleh, the legendary island in the Danube that had a mosque and minarets and was inhabited by a small community of Turks. They and the island's historic buildings were moved downstream.

Kazan gorge at its narrowest point. Danube at the narrowest point of the Iron Gates, seen from the Serbian side.
Sourced from Wikipedia Creative Commons: Photo author Dr. Konecsny Károly.

But Fermor's assertion that the lake extends almost to Baile Herculane is absurd as the baths are nearly ten miles from the river. As to the loss of beauty, current visitors to the Iron Gate will conclude that it is still exceedingly beautiful.

The next morning, coffee cup in hand, I strolled Orsova's embankment contemplating the amazing events that had occurred within the panorama before me. On the opposite Serbian shore invading Roman legions 20 centuries ago marched along a causeway built by 30,000 slaves. Often extending out over the water, its planks were supported by poles wedged into limestone cliffs. Excavation holes are still visible. An engineering marvel, in 103 A.D. the Via Traiana was commemorated with a tablet that has survived, even though it had to be moved higher when the dam arrived.

The Roman plaque "Tabula Traiana," Serbia
Sourced from Wikipedia Creative Commons: Photo by Rlichtefeld.

More recently in 1849 Hungarian revolutionary Lajos Kossuth and 4,000 of his defeated soldiers reached Orsova and crossed the river into Turkish territory where they were granted asylum by the sultan. Before fleeing Kossuth buried the 1,000-year-old jewel encrusted crown of the Hungarian kings beneath a willow tree on a bluff overlooking the Danube. Four years later the Austrians retrieved the crown and a grateful Franz Joseph built a shrine that is still there commemorating the recovery of the treasured relic.

Before the hydroelectric power plant, the 50-mile-long gorge (Kazan) culminated in the Iron Gate where the mighty river crashed through the narrows separating the Carpathians from the Balkan Mountains to the south. This treacherous stretch of water was a graveyard for boats and mariners. American writer

Bayard Taylor in 1859 described his perilous upstream passage through the Iron Gate:

> *Rocks had been blasted so as to afford a channel for the steamer, which trembles in every timber as she stems the foamy tangle of chutes and whirlpools. Let one of her iron muscles give way, and the river would have its will. A mile and a half of slow, trembling, exciting progress, and we had mounted the heaviest grade.*

Putting these thoughts aside I returned to my hotel, loaded the bike and set out amid a light rain to ride the short distance to the Iron Gate Dam. An hour later, past the industrial ruins that line the shore, I came to the power station. Here in 1972 Nicolai Ceausescu and Marshall Tito turned the switches inaugurating Europe's biggest hydroelectric dam. The billion-dollar project, seven years under construction, created locks that opened the Danube to year-round navigation.

I rode on hoping to find about a mile downstream the boat restaurant that I had visited in 1999 when I was reporting on NATO's air war against Yugoslavia. Silviu and Doina Tufis, Romanians who lived for a time in Australia, had purchased the worn-out river craft after the end of communism and were converting it to a restaurant and pension.

Soon I came upon a welcome billboard: "Boat Restaurant Vapor," 100 meters ahead. Coming around a bend I heard the lilting rhythms of Gypsy music coming from a loudspeaker. Arriving at the parking lot between the river and highway, I saw the repainted river craft tethered to the shore.

I approached the gangplank and asked for Doina. To my delight, a deckhand went off to find her. Emerging from the galley, she burst into a smile, as happy to see me as I was to see her. She insisted that I stay for lunch, an invitation I couldn't refuse.

Doina and her husband were fine, but the burden of running

a small business in post-communist Romania had taken a toll. Seated on the foredeck dining area with the sun shimmering on the Danube, we dined on cucumber and tomato salad and Bulgarian fish soup. Doina said business was brisk but that the stress of supervising a staff of 20 was heavy. "I'm a slave to my work," she complained, "when I'm doing one job my husband is doing another."

Me, Doina, and the Vapor boat restaurant

A band, she said, played on Fridays and Saturdays but the Gypsy musicians had stolen lanterns, a violin, and defaced posters. "We can't keep help," she continued, "they all want quick money and won't work. One girl had just left for Austria, two others to Germany, another to Italy." Their son Jimmy, who at 14 in 1999 had shown me the swans and ducks he kept in a roped off area adjacent to the boat, didn't finish high school and to his mother's dismay had run off to Australia.

Doina complained about Turkish truck drivers who she said parked their big rigs in the lot but didn't frequent the restaurant. "They want girls [prostitutes], but we don't do that, so they don't come in." She spoke of the bribes for permits that had to be paid to local authorities. Despite frustrations, she said, she and Silviu enjoyed what they're doing.

Declining Doina's invitation to stay overnight, I departed, wanting to travel six more miles to reach the town of Drobeta Turnu Severin.

It was 3 PM when I rode off, aware that I too had a problem. On the previous day's ride I had experienced pain in my left knee. It was the same injury that I had struggled with back in Lithuania. At Orsova the pain was so great that I had difficulty climbing the hotel stairs. The ride to the boat restaurant had been OK but now the knee hurt with every uphill grade.

Drobeta Turnu Severin is a transit town strung out along the contours of the river. I checked into the Continental Hotel, a modernist block overlooking the Danube where I had stopped in 1999. It was there that I had overheard negotiations—in English—about the price of diesel fuel being smuggled nightly into Serbia.

The town's name translates as "Severin's tower." It was here that the Roman bridge over the Danube crossed to the Dacian or Romanian shore. From the Iron Gate Museum situated in the town a visitor looks out at the still intact masonry footings of the bridge that for 1,000 years was the longest in the world.

Romanians—as evidenced by the name of their country— are proud of their connection to classical Rome. It's reflected in the many Italian words in their otherwise Slavic-based language. Their afternoon greeting sounds almost identical to the Italian, "buona sera." Good-bye in Romanian is "arevidera." Traian— Trajan—is a popular name for Romanian boys.

I hoped to reach Bulgaria the next day, but I worried that the throbbing knee would slow my progress and could cause the journey to be abandoned. Luckily Doru, the English-speaking druggist I met at the Ecco pharmacy in Severin, sug-gested a package of Advil. "Take two tablets now, and then again tomorrow, and see what happens," he said. Encouraged,

I mounted the bike and set out. Doru stepped outside to see me off, saying, "today you'll see how our farmers live, unchanged from medieval times."

It was 9:30 and 60 miles to the town of Calafat where I planned to cross the Danube by ferry to Vidin, Bulgaria. I chose the secondary road that followed the Danube for some miles before veering inland. Even as the countryside grew poorer, it was an exhilarating ride and miraculously there was no knee pain. Wildlife was abundant and for several miles I listened to croaking frogs, turkeys and geese. At Hinova I watched fishermen take their catches from the skiffs they took onto the Danube. A man in a John Deere cap with an uncle in Cleveland used both hands to hold up his biggest fish.

Two hours and 16 miles later I reached Rogova. The road had turned away from the river and the only people were farmers. The Banat hill country was far behind as the terrain was again flat and boring.

At a village in southern Romania

There was little traffic. I passed a woman on the side of the road. She bent beneath the weight of water buckets that hung from a pole she balanced on her shoulder. The women wore babooshkas, colorful aprons, leggings and sandals. They looked older than their years. When someone smiled, typically one or more teeth were missing. At 12:10 I passed Vanju Mare and then Receva, 26 miles from where I had started.

Sometimes I would pass a farm wagon pulled by a single horse with eye blinders and bells on the neck. Some wagon wheels were rubberized unlike the ones I saw in the Cerna Valley. On these wagons women typically sat cross-legged on a rug behind the driver.

Occasionally there were fine horses tethered in tall grass, their front legs joined with a rope so they moved only with short awkward jumps.

Rural Romania near Cetate and the Danube

The hours slid lazily by. At Cetate I watched old women cranking wooden buckets of water from deep municipal wells adjacent to the road. Mangy dogs slept on or near the road.

In late afternoon Adi telephoned from Timisoara and asked how I was doing. Telling him my location, he said, "today you're seeing the real Romania."

When I was within 15 miles of my destination, I took a break in the tiny village of Maglavit. Seated on a stoop next to the general store, I took out my pocket notebook and recorded data—

time, speed, places and the usual things I like to remember. That task completed, I placed the notebook and pen on the post next to the stoop and walked to a trash barrel to discard containers and wrappers. At that point three or four boys came by kicking a soccer ball. I was distracted and rode off without the notebook. A mile down the road I was startled to discover it wasn't in my vest pocket. Remembering at once where I had left it, I made a U-turn and headed back to Maglavit. To my relief the notebook with names and phone numbers I needed was still there.

My route through Romania and Bulgaria

I reached dusty, drab Calafat at 6:45 PM, completing a seven-hour, 60-mile ride.

Aside from a solitary textile factory there was little activity in Calafat. The downtown, such as it was, was dreary and bereft of people. Arriving at the ferry dock, a chain had already been pulled across the entrance, a sign that I had missed the hourly departure. Just then a guard came out of the kiosk, took down the chain, and pointed to his watch telling me to hurry. Taking a remaining wad of Romanian lei from my pocket I quickly purchased a ticket, had my passport stamped, and raced down the ramp where the barge was still tethered to the shore.

Once aboard I parked the bike behind a tractor-trailer that bore the comforting "CZ" sticker for the Czech Republic. As the engine groaned and the barge slipped away from dock, I observed several people behind me reaching into cloth bags and removing cartons of cigarettes. They hastily tore away wrappers, which they hurled into the river. The small time smugglers attracted no attention from Romanian and Bulgarian customs officers on either side of the Danube.

# VII.

# BULGARIA and MACEDONIA

Reaching Bulgaria was a milestone. It was my third crossing of the Danube—first from Slovakia to Hungary, then in the middle of Hungary, and now deep in the Balkans from Romania to Vidin in the land of the Bulgars.

Bulgaria is a challenge for cyclists because of its mountains and the additional problem of the Cyrillic alphabet. Unlike Serbia that uses Cyrillic but also Latin script, in rural Bulgaria signs are often Cyrillic only. These factors plus grinding poverty and the absence of much English create an awkward sense of being at the farthest edge of Europe.

Knowing expert cyclists who abandoned their journeys in Bulgaria, I'd come to regard the country as a graveyard for cycling dreams.

When the barge bumped against the dock, car and truck engines sputtered to life while pedestrians strode quickly to the gangway. Customs formalities were easy and efficient, even for the cigarette smugglers. A couple of minutes later I was riding off in search of a place to stay. The Andel (Star) Hotel appeared to be a natural. It was modern with newer cars bearing foreign license plates in the lot.

Locking the bike, I ventured inside. The front desk clerk spoke English but said a power outage meant that for the moment he couldn't process credit cards. Another American behind me stepped forward and said he would lend me Bulgarian leva until I got money from the cash machine around the corner.

My generous countryman from Maryland said he was part of a group of chiropractors doing missionary work. He said they were hosting a free medical clinic in the town center.

At breakfast the next morning an Indian American from New York, whose firm sourced clothing from multiple locations, said he was in Vidin to close his Bulgaria factory. Its production, he said, would shift to Costa Rica, closer to the U.S. market. About 1,000 Vidin workers would lose their jobs. For textiles and apparel, he said, Bulgaria had become too expensive and too distant from the U.S. The workers here, he said, were earning less than $100 per month.

Apartment building, Vidin

Having completed a good day on Romania's back roads, I hoped for a similar result going south from Vidin. With what I thought to be a good map, I chose secondary roads that hugged the Danube for 15 miles and then veered southeast through lowlands before joining the main road to Montana, my next destination.

The route was challenging. There were potholes and uneven surfaces. One stretch was so rough that my left pannier shook loose and bounced to the pavement. The signage—all in Cyrillic—was spotty and I often wasn't sure I was on the right road. But the weather was agreeable and there was little traffic. At the village of Arber I bid farewell to the Danube and took a ten-minute break entertained by a stork constructing a nest on top of a telephone pole.

Passing through more destitute villages—Topolovitz, Brusarci and Slavotin—it was depressing to see people in such dire circumstances. Most farm wagons did not have rubber tires and were pulled by donkeys. I grew tired of seeing men and women pawing through trash barrels. After eight boring, frustrating hours, I arrived in Montana, a medium-size town 50 miles from Vidin.

Farm wagon without rubber tires, northern Bulgaria

Montana's population was 40,000 but it was poor like the surrounding countryside. Demoralized by pervasive poverty, I was eager to reach Sofia, which was still two days away. I dined alone that evening in a Chinese restaurant, asking myself what was I doing in northern Bulgaria.

My spirits lifted in the morning when at breakfast I met a young man who spoke English. Ivan Milchev was 26, a salesman for a Greek-owned bank in Sofia. He had driven to Montana in his company car, an Opel Corsa. His job was getting bank customers to use credit cards. He conceded the task was formidable as people were getting by on about $100 per month. Why would such people want a credit card or be good credit risks, I asked. Ivan shrugged.

As Ivan told his story, it was apparent that Bulgaria's market economy was working for him. In addition to the company car, he owned a late model Spanish Seat. Ivan was too young to remember communism. He earned $600 per month and from that he was able to save something. His territory was rural western and northern Bulgaria. He wasn't discouraged by the low incomes. "Even though their income is low," he said, "they may use a credit card to buy furniture or mobile phones."

I departed Montana clinging to a hope that perhaps I could make Sofia in a single day but I soon realized that was impossible. The riding was too difficult and my load felt heavier than usual. And my pace was greatly restrained by the mountainous terrain. I would climb for an hour and then rest. Only when big trucks rumbled past was I sure I was still on the right road.

I began to think that I too could be defeated by Bulgaria. In the town of Vratsa I saw my first Bulgarian train, a sign that I hoped suggested modernity ahead. I passed Mezdra and after more hours of hard riding came to Botevgrad. Given the frequent climbs, I had made good time, coming 50 miles in eight hours. It was six PM.

In Botevgrad my spirits brightened as I was within reach of Sofia, which was only 36 miles away. Searching for a hotel, on the spur of the moment I stopped at the bus station. I began to wonder if I could leave the bike and go by bus to Sofia and then return in the morning to ride to the capital. This would allow both for a survey of the roadway and a good night's rest in a better hotel. I could even take some of my heavy gear and leave it at a Sofia hotel.

The bus station was crowded but not chaotic. At the inter-city window a clerk spoke English. She said there was a bus for Sofia in 45 minutes and several returning in the morning. Elated, I purchased a round trip ticket for the equivalent of $2.00. Now all I needed was a safe place to leave the bike.

Riding out from the bus station, I sought out the most modern hotel, parked, and approached the front desk. I told my story and the young bilingual woman in charge replied at once, "lock the bike at the employee entrance at the back where it will be safe. I'll be on duty when you return tomorrow." Her words were music to my ears. Moments later I handed this wonderful person my two panniers and handlebar bag for safekeeping and departed.

Just being aboard a bus headed for the capital boosted my spirits. However that glow quickly faded when I observed the formidable climb the bus was making just getting out of town. Higher mountains were ahead. Implausibly, I thought, I would be traveling on a four-lane highway through the tallest moun-tains I had yet seen. I learned later that this highway was a prized infrastructure project of Bulgaria's last communist government.

Soon we were in the outskirts of Sofia. There was new con-struction that made Sofia look like a boomtown instead of the sleepy Balkan capital that I had known in the 1990s.

Dropped off in the center of Sofia, I found a good hotel, checked in and treated myself to a steak dinner served on a white tablecloth with starched napkins. My waiter, a young edu-cated boy called Mihail, responded to my complimenting his English by saying English was no longer an advantage, it was essential in getting a job.

Refreshed and rejuvenated, the next morning at 8 AM I was on a bus back to Botevgrad. Arriving, I walked to the hotel where the friendly clerk was on duty as promised. Giving her a generous tip, I unlocked the bike, loaded up, and began what I knew would be an arduous journey to Sofia.

Despite knowing from two bus rides what I was getting into, the riding was even more challenging than I anticipated and at times it was frightening. There was the steep climb coming out of Botevgrad, but once on the freeway I encountered magnificent bridges that spanned deep valleys. On these bridges the winds were often so strong that I was in fear of being blown over. The bike swayed in the wind even though my speed was minimal. More than once I nearly lost control. Stopping on a bridge to adjust a brake pad, I became dizzy just looking over the railing. Far below I watched a hawk gliding on the currents in wide circles above the forest.

In addition to the wind there were long tunnels. From the bus I had been unable to detect the extent to which the shoulders narrowed inside the tunnels, which were totally dark. Even though I switched on my lights, I worried that passing cars and trucks wouldn't see me. I also worried that police patrols could chase me away from the highway saying bicycles weren't allowed. Back in the open the downhill runs were frightening. At times I traveled so fast that I was terrified. Often I touched the brakes to slow down and maintain control.

But the ride went steadily on. At 1 PM I came out of a third tunnel to find a sign saying Sofia was only 12 miles away. By three PM I passed Sofia airport with majestic Mt. Vitosha off to the left. Sofia, to those who haven't visited, is unique in Eastern Europe in having a 1,500-meter mountain hovering above it.

Soon I was in the city center and returned again to the Crystal Palace Hotel where I had spent the previous night. It was 4 PM and I felt triumph that I had actually reached Sofia on a bicycle.

Delighted at the prospect of a second night in a sparkling Sofia, I spent an enjoyable hour visiting downtown sites. Streets and buildings had been renovated. There were smart restaurants and new hotels in the center.

Alexander Nevsky Cathedral, Sofia, Bulgaria

Sofia's monumental core is a tableau of Bulgarian history. There's the iconic Alexander Nevsky Cathedral honoring its orthodox Christianity and fraternal links to Russia. The church bears the name of Russian Czar Alexander II's patron saint. Alexander's army drove the Turks from Bulgaria in 1878. A large equestrian statue of Czar Alexander stands in parliament square, its elaborate frieze depicting Russian Cossacks putting the sword to heathen Turks.

Farther on is Sofia's unique yellow brick road, golden paving stones from Vienna—a 1907 gift of Emperor Franz Joseph to his cousin, Bulgaria's Prince Ferdinand. Amazingly in the 1990s Ferdinand's grandson, Simeon II, returned from exile in Spain and was elected to serve four years as Bulgaria's reformist prime minister.

Yellow brick road with the former royal palace on the right

After days of hard riding I was eager to reach Macedonia, across more mountains to the west.

At 10:30 on a Friday morning I rode out from Sofia. Traffic was heavy with trucks bound for the port of Thessaloniki, Greece. It was 12 miles before the E79 highway veered south while I stayed on Route 6 headed southwest.

Sofia's western hinterland is a dreary collection of industrial towns, a string of derelict communist-era factories, one after another. While in this wasteland I came close to disaster. A road crew was pouring blacktop and I joined a line of cars and trucks approaching the old steel-making town of Pernik.

On a steep downhill a slow moving communist-era double trailer truck swung into the passing lane and lumbered past me. The trailer's rear reflector that extended out to the side came within inches of my head. I swerved onto the shoulder that was topped with several inches of sand. Speeding into that alien surface, the bike tipped dangerously right and then left. Only with difficulty did I maintain stability. Had I gone down I would have fallen onto the roadway and death or serious injury would have been the result. I believe I was spared by luck, a balanced front load, and by the firm grip of wide-diameter tires.

I reached Pernik at 12:30 and 30 minutes later equally decaying Radomir. Then the mountains began. Regrettably my topographical map was accurate as I had entered the area of darkest color, meaning elevations of 1,200 meters and higher. Climbing, I stopped often to regain strength and revive my flagging spirit.

I had traveled this highway before, but again from a car one doesn't get a true sense of terrain. I could see that the tallest mountains were ahead, nearer the Macedonian border. As the ride proceeded, I began having mental lapses, a sure sign of fatigue. At one stop I neglected to zip up the case on the rear rack. Another time I failed to attach the straps on the trunk. Such mistakes can be fatal.

But I had also had successes. I was now well beyond Sofia and I had not been defeated by Bulgaria. Determined to reach Macedonia I had to climb these Balkan summits. I told myself if I could reach the border at Kriva Palanka things would be better. From Kriva Palanka it would essentially be a downhill run into Macedonia's Vardar Valley and then a straightaway southwest to the capital of Skopje.

But for now I was in mountains and maximum physical effort was required.

At 2 PM I reached Izvor and then crossed a lower summit near Konjavo at 3:30. I had traveled only eight miles in 1½ hours.

Not only was the riding physically demanding, it was cold. I put on gloves to warm my hands.

Finally in the distance I could see Kustendil, the last Bulgarian town before the border. But then, gazing at even taller mountains to the west, I was discouraged. While a day earlier, I celebrated arriving in Sofia, now I contemplated overnighting in Kustendil, abandoning the goal of reaching Macedonia that day. Even though the maps told me the border was only 13 miles beyond Kustendil, I was finished. I wasn't about to test fate on another climb just to reach another country.

Absorbed by these thoughts, I realized that I was still well short of Kustendil. Luckily, there were now long downhills as well as climbs. One descent went on for five miles. Downhills in high mountains and cold temperatures present another set of problems. A tough climb creates enough body sweat that soaks a tee shirt. But speeding downhill the rushing wind presses wet clothing against the skin and the body gets cold. In addition the riding was rough as the road surface was uneven. I had learned that the Bulgarians often put gravel over the macadam and that creates a hard and perilous ride. By 4:15 I was still three miles short of Kustendil. Finally at 5:00 PM I rolled into the town center. It had been a horrid day, six hours of the hardest riding yet. And I had covered a mere 42 miles.

While I felt satisfaction upon reaching Kustendil, I was cold, tired and unsure of what to do. Should I stop or try to struggle up another mountain the 13 miles to the border? As I rode through the town, Kustendil was not without attraction. It had Roman thermal baths and a hotel that looked decent. I was tempted to stay. All the while, I contemplated what I thought was the Bulgarian curse of being defeated by fatigue and tall mountains, of petering out and having ultimately to give up.

As usual, I assessed my options outside a small store with a sit-down break for yogurt and carbonated water. Examining my maps I dropped the idea of riding on. It was time to stop. But instead of settling on a decision to stay in Kustendil, I decided to check one more option, whether there might be an evening bus to Macedonia. I rode off in search of the bus station.

At the edge of town at an open-air market I spotted a well-dressed young woman next to a fruit stand. Assuming she would speak English, I asked directions. She answered in perfect

English and said that while she was from Sofia, she was pretty sure the bus station was just one block farther west. I thanked her and rode on.

While at the kiosk inquiring about schedules, a tall, thin middle-aged man politely asked in English if he could be of assistance. His name was Mihail Spassov. He said he was the father of the young woman at the fruit stand. Mihail was rough-cut with long graying hairs extending from the back of his neck. He was a Bulgarian diplomat assigned to Kosovo and was returning there after picking up his family in Sofia. They were paying him a visit over a long holiday weekend. Mihail then asked, "Would you like to ride with us to Macedonia?" He said there was room for the bike in the back of their Opel sedan. Immediately I said yes.

Just like that my plans had changed. While Mihail's wife and daughter walked back to the greengrocer's to get more things, he and I set to work unloading the bike, removing the front wheel, and then rearranging luggage in the back of the family Opel. With the wheel off the bike and my gear could be squeezed on top of duffle bags and family suitcases. The task accomplished, we picked up the two women with their cucumbers, tomatoes and onions and were off. Thus began an unexpected but immensely satisfying three-hour journey.

Reaching the border Mihail steered into the diplomatic lane and we were waved through without inspection. Kriva Palanka offers an extraordinary panorama of the surrounding mountains. Snow was visible on the tallest peaks.

The three Spassovs were fluent in English and the conversation flowed easily. Mihail's reserved, refined wife was a prosecuting attorney in Sofia. The daughter Biljana was 16 and studied at Sofia's French language lyceum. An older sister was a graduate student in Paris.

When I asked Biljana what she would like to be doing in five years, she replied, "living in France or Switzerland." This prompted the parents to exchange a hurried glance that I took to be surprise and satisfaction. The family agreed that the current period was probably the best ever in Bulgaria's long, troubled history. I was not surprised when Mihail spoke derisively of Bulgaria having endured 500 years "under the Turkish yoke." It was an expression I had heard often.

Then the wife's reserve gave way to animation as she explained that 50 years of communism had wreaked havoc with Bulgaria's proud heritage in literature and art. She apologized for her reticence in English saying she was more comfortable in French.

Mihail was a U.S. enthusiast. He asserted that our problems would be solved because we so openly discuss them. The United States, he continued, was the last hope for mankind.

Having gained an hour crossing into Macedonia, at 7 PM we came to Kumanovo, the substantial city not far from the capital of Skopje. Mihail drove to the busy bus station. Shooing away beggars we lifted the disassembled bike out of the back and reattached the wheel and seat post. Bidding my new friends a fond farewell, they drove off north to Kosovo.

Exhausted, I pushed the bike into the bus station and purchased a ticket for Skopje.

The short bus journey took me along the freeway that comes south from Belgrade and goes all the way to the Greek border. Its construction was a considerable engineering feat and highly prized in Tito's Yugoslavia because it opened up the impoverished southern sections of the country.

I'm no stranger to Skopje as I spent many weeks there during the several years of war that followed the breakup of Yugoslavia. Arriving at the familiar Holiday Inn on the south bank of the Vardar River, I locked the bike and checked in.

At this point I broke off my journey and didn't return until some months later.

Wedged between Greece and Serbia, Macedonia is a hard luck country. Since independence in 1991 the nation of two million has confronted implacable hostility from Athens, which claims exclusive right to the name Macedonia, which is a region of northern Greece. Alexander the Great (356-323 B.C.) came from Greek Macedonia, and Slavic Macedonians—contrary to their assertions—have no direct connection to him. Greek opposition keeps Macedonia out of NATO and blocks its progress towards the European Union.

Macedonia has always been a Balkans crossroads. Here the east-west Roman road from the Adriatic to Byzantium (Constantinople) met the north-south road from the Slavic lands to the Aegean Sea. Macedonia has been fought over for centuries.

Isak Ramadani

When I arrived back in Skopje I called my friend Isak Ramadani, a fellow journalist, and we agreed to meet for dinner. Isak, an ethnic Albanian whose family has deep roots in Skopje, suggested a restaurant in the old town. Over the phone soft-spoken Isak surprised me, declaring, "why don't we dine like pashas this evening?" Thus we made our way through narrow lanes on the north side of the Vardar to a Turkish restaurant where we reclined on cushions and settled into a wonderful evening of food, laughter and stimulating conversation. Over the years I've learned so much from Isak about the history of Albanians in the former Yugoslavia.

The next day Isak generously offered to drive me back to the Bulgarian border near to where I had halted my ride.

So at 9 AM on a misty autumn morning we loaded the Cannondale into Isak's Volkswagen and headed east for Kriva Palanka where we arrived an hour and a half later.

My route through Macedonia

Bidding my friend a sincere thank you, at a filling station on the edge of town I assembled the bike and packed the load. Then I purchased sparkling water and yogurt. Setting the odometer, I was nine miles west of the Bulgarian border and a further 20 miles from Kustendil. My destination was Kumanovo, the ethnically mixed town where my Bulgarian friends had dropped me off the previous spring. Amid a light rain, I set off.

As I rode, I contemplated how this road for centuries was the principal route between Turkey and the Balkans. In 1389 the Islamic army of Sultan Murad, heading for their victory over the Christians in Kosovo, must have trod this very road.

I was two hours into the ride, still thinking of the uneasy relations between Christians and Muslims in the Balkans, when the rain turned heavy. I had to put the rain covers over the panniers and don my foul weather gear. Soaked, I eventually found shelter at a roadside café whose sign depicted a cup of steaming coffee. An arrow directed me up a short hill to a house where smoke curled up from the chimney. Stepping inside, I hung my dripping poncho on a peg and sat at a metal table whose legs grated on the concrete floor. In this smoky refuge, I tried to converse with the man I took to be the owner who sat at an adjacent table with a young girl I assumed was his daughter. A woman, presumably the wife and mother, stood behind the counter. She eventually arrived with a demitasse cup of Turkish coffee on a red metal tray. Fast cadenced Turkish music, popular everywhere in the Balkans, played loudly from the radio.

Outside the rain fell harder and I was glad to have found warmth and shelter. Attempting to communicate with my hosts, I asked the woman if she spoke English. She waved a dismissive finger and said, "ruski." That wouldn't work for me so I countered asking if she could do German or French. "Klein bischen Deutsch," was the reply and after that we made progress. Her name was Tamara and her daughter was seven. She had been a teacher at the Russian language school in Kumanovo but it had closed some years earlier, leaving her without an income. Her husband, she continued, worked irregularly. The family, she said, lived at a higher level prior to Macedonia becoming independent. Now, she said, the family subsisted on the meager earnings from the café. "Yugoslavia," she said in English, "very good."

Some minutes later when I stepped outside and flicked away the puddles from the tops of the panniers, trunk and seat, I felt a wave of contentment. I was smiling because despite temporary discomfort I love being in the Balkans. There is something mysterious and compelling about Gypsy music, Turkish coffee, the world's best yogurt, and challenging conversations in disparate languages. In short, I was delighted to be back in Macedonia, a remote place that I find at once to be familiar and exotic.

Resuming the journey, the rain fell harder. Oncoming vehicles had their lights on. By 6:15 PM it was dark. A road sign announced that Kumanovo was only six miles away but the remaining time passed slowly.

I became preoccupied with my physical discomfort. I was soaked. There were puddles at the tips of my gloves. My shoes were likes sponges. The pools of water at the toes slid to the heels and then back with each turn of the pedals. Headlights of approaching cars illuminated sheets of rain bouncing off the pavement.

Spotting a bus shelter, I took refuge. While there an eastbound bus stopped across the road and four men tumbled out and stood in a line peeing to leeward of the downpour.

Finally the rain eased and I rode slowly on. Soon I saw the lights of Kumanovo. Twenty minutes later, cold and wet, I rode through deserted streets and came to the Hotel Parigi. They had a room. I took it and shifted my mind to the prospect of a hot shower, dry clothes and a restaurant meal. At ten PM I sat alone in the hotel dining room, dry and refreshed, and enjoyed a wonderful meal of soup, Srpski salad, and spaghetti Bolognese.

The next morning the sky had cleared. But my gear was still

wet, particularly my shoes, which I strapped to the trunk hoping the sun would dry them. The ride from the Bulgarian border to Kumanovo had been the worst, most uncomfortable day I had yet experienced.

Skopje, Stone Bridge over the Vardar

After some time I arrived in Skopje but I paused only long enough to say farewell to friends and gaze again at the wonderful Kale fortress above the old Turkish Stone Bridge over the Vardar that dates from the 1400s.

I rode south on the wide shoulder of the freeway headed for Veles. I was fearful of being stopped by police who might invoke a rule that bikes were not permitted on Macedonian freeways. The traffic was mostly trucks headed for Greece. Gradually the mountains ahead of me rose higher, taller even than those between Sofia and the Macedonian border. There was recurrent climbing and unlit tunnels. One was a quarter mile in length and pitch black inside. I switched on my meager lights and navigated from the headlights of approaching vehicles. I was vulnerable and felt stupid for being inadequately equipped. Outside the tunnel the roadway was flung so high up that a slip through the rudimentary stone barriers would mean death in the canyon below.

At 8 PM I reached Veles, a provincial town and railway center, a long 40 miles from Kumanovo. Dropping down onto the side road I passed shepherds tending sheep, goats and cows. They carried handcrafted staffs and wore colorful knitted caps and vests. I stopped to watch a man cutting grass with a scythe that he skillfully swung from side to side. His slow, easy motion would have been unchanged through centuries. I was back in a rural environment where life proceeded at the slow pace I became accustomed to in Romania and Bulgaria.

Rebecca West, the renowned English writer traveling in 1937 with her husband, another couple and a driver in a grand automobile, stopped in Veles to gather material for her masterful two-volume work on Yugoslavia, *Black Lamb, Grey Falcon.* West loved Yugoslavia, particularly Macedonia, which she called "the most beautiful land I had ever seen in my life." At Veles, among other observations, she spoke of the fragrance of acacia trees in late summer:

> *The air was... flavored, it was dense with the essence of flowers. It was Veles that we were approaching, a town that a great many people admire on their way to Athens: its elegant dilapidated Turkish houses, painted in refined colors, hang on each side of a rocky gorge cleft by the rushing Vardar.*

I pedaled into town thinking what a sensation that her massive Lincoln must have caused in 1937. The Turkish houses still hang on the sides of the gorge but they're run down and bereft of color.

The hotel I found, The Veles, backed up on the Vardar, whose rushing waters were an audio backdrop as I parked and went inside. It had been a good day even though I hadn't covered much territory. My odometer registered 40 miles, but the riding had been tough and I hadn't departed Kumanovo until 2 PM.

After emptying the panniers and laying out clothing and shoes that were now dry, I returned to the lobby, drawn by the lilting Gypsy music that rose from the lower level. Venturing down carpeted stairs, the music grew louder. Prying open a tall door, a virtual wall of sound and body heat rushed out. Inside dozens of dark-skinned people, sweat streaming from their faces, stood in lines and circles, swaying hypnotically to the rhythms of an orchestra in which a clarinet and saxophone were dominant. I learned later that the revelers were Turkish, Gypsy (Romany) and Albanian. The dancing went on until midnight.

The next morning I was awakened early by a clatter outside the window. Pulling open the drapes, I saw hundreds of black birds swarming in a large willow trees next to the fast flowing, brown river. The cackling and commotion went on for 30 minutes. Then, as quickly as they arrived, the large birds took flight and it was quiet.

After a buffet breakfast I spread out maps and contemplated the day ahead. My first priority was finding a bike shop. One of my high gears was slipping and the rear brakes gripped unevenly. Making enquiries at the front desk, I was directed to the Pony Bike Shop where the proprietor, Kiro, immediately set to work without more than a visual prompting from me as to what was wrong. His equipment was primitive, but he knew his craft and within minutes the bike stood upright, ready to ride.

I was aware that I was heading into tall mountains, no matter if I went southwest over a secondary road to Prilep or continued south along the Vardar and then turned west where the map suggested there was a more substantial road. I chose the second route through Gradsko and it was a mistake. Thus began a most frustrating day.

Kiro's Pony bicycle shop in Veles

Proceeding south along the old road adjacent to the river, I wasn't 10 minutes past Veles before there was trouble. Aware of a clicking from the rear tire, I stopped. Rotating the wheel, I discovered a thorn protruding from the tread. Removing the load, I tried to pull out the thorn but it broke apart. I then used my teeth to extract its point from the tread. I pumped in air, reloaded, and pressed on. A mile farther on the rear tire was flat. It was already 1 PM. Over the next hour, I worked fitfully on the repair—first not finding the mark I made in the flattened tube, and then the patch failed to adhere.

Discouraged, seated by the roadside, I witnessed a kind of miracle. Three fast-moving cyclists in racing garb came over a hill headed my way. They stopped, introduced themselves, assessed my situation, and went to work. Not one of them spoke English. After a new patch was applied, the tall rider, Nikola, in a yellow jersey and racing cap, took out his pump and furiously pumped away. Moments later he was bouncing the inflated tire on the pavement. It was a job that I hadn't carried out in 60 minutes. They had done it in ten minutes. The trio of riders then remounted, waved, and rode off, leaving me to think I had been visited by guardian angels in remotest Macedonia.

I rode on and eventually reached Gradsko where the road to Prilep went off to the west. I stopped at a Makpetrol Station for provisions and fell into conversation with a youngish man named Dean, who had learned English from working in Sweden. He was exceedingly bitter and from his lips tumbled a litany of complaints about corrupt politicians, low wages, and how foreigners—Germans and Greeks mostly—were buying up Macedonia's assets on the cheap. But Dean's real message was about the arduous ride ahead of me. He said that before Prilep there was a 13-mile climb up Pletvar, the tallest mountain in this region. Dean then directed me to a modern bed and break-fast on a farm nearby. I took his advice and went to the B&B.

Spreading my maps out on the bed, calculator in my hand, I was filled with consternation. On this horrid day, I had cov-ered only half the distance I had targeted and hadn't reached the steepest climbs. I had traveled a pathetic 22 miles from Veles and it was 30 miles more to reach Prilep and then another 30 miles to Bitola. That meant that in order to reach Tirana, Albania and my scheduled flight home I needed to cover 60 miles the next day over the tallest mountains I had yet encountered. Folding the maps and putting them away, for the first time I doubted that I could finish the trip.

In the morning I was refreshed and determined to take my best shot, both in conquering Pletvar and reaching Bitola. At 7:30 I began loading the bike for the long day ahead. There was modest fog but it appeared likely to lift. After coffee and a light breakfast, I set out, stopping first at the village store where I purchased a larger than usual supply of bread, fruit and carbonated water. The friendly young woman behind the counter did a brisk business but it was apparent that her clientele were struggling financially.

It was 9:30 when I departed from Rosoman. My attention was focused on the climb up the 3,200-foot-high Pletvar, one of the most difficult mountain passes in Macedonia. In Tour de France terms, Pletvar would be at least a category two climb.

The first hour wasn't bad. The terrain was mostly flat and I covered 11 miles. Then the serious climbing began. I climbed continually for the next hour and traveled six miles. At 12:25 PM, with sweat pouring from my face and dripping from my helmet, the shirt beneath my old red wool sweater soaked, I was at Trojac. It was the hardest riding yet. A sign pointed to a 1,745-meter mountain to the left. Rain was now threatening. After one more hour, at 1:30 PM, I reached Pletvar's summit. I passed a sign that declared the elevation was 998 meters.

I had traveled 22 miles in four hours. Pausing at the summit to wring the sweat from my shirt and put on a dry one, I could see ahead and below the town of Prilep and the productive agricultural valley that adjoins it. Far away, trucks that looked tiny were headed my way, climbing the mountain from the Prilep side.

It took an hour to come down, miles slipped away without effort. I sped along, sometimes touching 30 miles per hour. Reaching the valley floor my odometer registered 36 miles. It was 2:30 in the afternoon. Satisfied with what I had accomplished, I turned mildly optimistic. If the road south was smooth and without major climbs, perhaps I could indeed reach Bitola before dark.

Now on level land I was in Macedonia's agricultural heartland. Famous for gigantic red peppers, the newly harvested vegetables were set out on racks, offered to passing motorists from almost every farmhouse.

Pletvar, from Prilep

The Bitola road was smooth and there wasn't much traffic. At 3:30 PM I was hungry, thirsty and in need of a break. Seeing the sign for the village of Topolcani, I diverted from the highway and rode a quarter mile west into extreme poverty. The village was decrepit, its single street rutted and unpaved. Storefronts were boarded up. Finding an open shop, I was able to purchase bread, cheese and mineral water. I sat in a broken plastic chair in front of the store and observed a dispiriting tableau. A disabled man on crutches hobbled slowly past. A drunken beggar approached muttering in German that there was no money and no work. An old man driving a donkey cart with a half load of twigs rattled past. A young mother pushed a wheelbarrow that was her stroller, the young child clutching its dirty edges.

Back on the road, I put Topolcani's poverty aside and focused on my apparent success in reaching my goal. After another 90 minutes at 5:30 PM I reached the cobblestones of Bitola's northern suburbs. I had done it. I had ridden 61 miles and conquered Pletvar in the process. I had reached renowned Bitola, Macedonia's second largest city situated not far from the border with Greece. Approaching the center, there were narrow lanes, a street bazaar, a languid canal, and a busy square where a mosque and a church shared opposite corners. There were old buildings in the traditional Turkish style where the second floor extends out over the first. It was a fantastic feeling to be in Bitola.

With its Albanian sweet shops and bakeries, Turkish veneer, and diverse population, Bitola created an immediate impression that people of different cultures can peacefully coexist.

Completing my most satisfying day of riding yet, I was delighted to find the De Niro Hotel that occupied two floors above a restaurant of the same name. Its owner, I discovered, was a great fan of the film star, Robert De Niro. My room was fit for a pasha, beautifully furnished with handcrafted wooden tables and chairs, parquet flooring, a modern bath, and a ladder that ascended to an upper level sleeping loft. Double-hung casement windows opened above an interior garden.

The walls of the pizza restaurant below displayed photographs from the First World War, when Bitola—then called Monastir—sheltered the allied French and Serbian troops who held out against the siege of the Austrians, Germans and Bulgars in the surrounding mountains. This was the Salonika front where there was fierce fighting. Also displayed was a 1917 postcard that must not have been mailed. It was addressed to a mother back in Paris and signed, "votre fils, Philip."

Trifun, the headwaiter, had the confident bearing of a successful businessman. When other customers had departed he shared his opinions on what was happening in his country where unemployment exceeded 30%. "We have been waiting in vain through 15 years of independence for our lives to improve," he began. "Our political system," he said, "is rotten and our politicians corrupt. They play games in the capital and line their own pockets." He continued, "We are two million Macedonians working so that 200 people in Skopje can be rich." It was the same complaint I had heard from Dean back in Gradsko.

Trifun at the Bitola pizza restaurant

Bitola

In the morning I strolled the pleasant streets of Bitola and reflected on another dissatisfied son of the town, Mustafa Kemal, later to be known as Ataturk (father), the revolutionary founder of post-Ottoman Turkey. Kemal Ataturk was born south of Bitola closer to Salonika. But of course this entire region—Rumelia—was part European Turkey. Ataturk came to Monastir at age 15 in 1896 and graduated from the military high school three years later. As I walked along the city's canal, I imagined that his enlightenment ideals had been nurtured in charming Monastir/Bitola.

Inspired by Bitola's cultural mix and still aglow from what I had achieved the previous day, I took my time. But as much as I wished to stay longer, I had to get going. I was already skeptical about what I feared was Trifun's optimistic assessment of the relative ease of getting over Bukovo to Lake Ohrid, my next destination. I've learned that non-cyclists who travel a route by car often misjudge a climb. Trifun had said there were only two very manageable mountains ahead of me, "maybe three kilometers up, nothing like the 24 km you had with Pletvar." I hoped he was right but my map said that Bukovo was 1,207 meters, considerably higher than Pletvar.

Before describing my harrowing climb over Bukovo in which I came perilously close to death, here's a quick word about yogurt. In their half millennia in the Balkans, the Turks clearly did much that was bad but also considerable good. They brought coffee to Europe, and also yogurt.

I first encountered this extraordinary dairy product in the 1960s as a graduate student in Yugoslavia. I've been a yogurt aficionado ever since. Yogurt in the Balkans is the real thing and not sugared up. It is bracing, thick, with an edge, and sold at reasonable prices.

* * *

It was 11:45 AM when I rode out from Bitola. Almost immediately the landscape changed. The rocky cliffs were gone, replaced by dense pine and hardwood forests. Red apples were being harvested from orchards at the lower elevations. It was only a few miles before I entered the mountains where the riding became challenging. In two hours I traveled 12 miles. Continuing at that pace I reached the town of Resen. I had already been up one 990-meter-high pass and the road was so high that I could see Lake Prespa off to the south on the border with Greece.

At 3:50 PM a sign indicated a steep climb over the next two and a half miles. I was headed up a 1,207-meter mountain. A man on a tractor turned onto the highway from an orchard, passed me, and gestured for me to take an apple from the stack on his wagon. I did, and the stranger's gesture diverted my mind from the ordeal of the climb. At 4:20 PM I reached the summit where a sign declared, "Bukovo, 1,190 meters."

Once again, I felt a brief feeling of triumph. There was a forester's cabin at the top and a parking lot where truckers adjusted the canvasses that covered their loads. Everything around me was green. Hawks circled below. It was cold. Despite that, I removed my windbreaker, fleece and shirt that was drenched with sweat. I put on fresh clothes, knowing from my experience on Pletvar that there would be a cold wind going downhill.

The run down was exhilarating. At times my speed touched 30 miles per hour. For two miles my feet were stationary on the pedals. I kept a wary eye out for irregularities in the pavement, my fingertips coiled over the brakes. I watched for approaching cars that could force me off the road. There was no shoulder.

I couldn't believe what happened next. An older white Opel coming up the mountain veered into my lane to pass a truck. It came straight at me. Terrified, I instantly realized what I was up against. Time stood still. The driver of the Opel probably didn't even see me. In milliseconds I concluded that my only hope was to hold tight on the handlebar grips and steer as close as possible to the edge of the roadway. In a flash the Opel hurtled past me. My eyes remained fixed on the road. The bike shook from the wind of the speeding car and its throbbing engine roared in my ears. Gulping for air and trying to slow down, I realized I was upright and stable.

I kept moving until it seemed safe to firmly apply the brakes and stop. Only then did my limbs tremble, a trembling that lasted several minutes. Did the Opel miss me by six inches, 12 inches, 18 inches, two feet? I'll never know. What I do know is that this near miss on Bukovo was the closest I've ever come to death.

Still shaken, at 4:40 PM I reached the base of Bukovo. I had traveled 31 miles. I continued on and asked a man standing in his front yard the distance to Ohrid. His reply of "chetteri" (four) kilometers was a pleasant surprise as I assumed it was much farther. At 5:30 PM I was in the town center and checked into the hotel recommended by my friends in Bitola.

Ohrid and its lake are jewels, hidden gems about which Rebecca West observed in 1937 that "not one Englishman in a million has ever been to Ohrid." For orthodox Macedonians Ohrid is the spiritual heart of the country. It was here in the 9th century that Saint Clement, a principal disciple of the Greek brothers Saints Cyril and Methodius who brought Christianity to the Slavs, developed the Cyrillic alphabet. Clement founded Ohrid's Literary School, paving the way for a millennium of monastic study. The town is wonderfully situated on a hill above the northern shore of Lake Ohrid, the deepest lake in Europe, 18 miles in length with its southern parts forming Macedonia's borders with Albania and Greece.

Because of its unique geography and tall mountains, banks of fog often settle over Ohrid, adding to its appeal. Like Bitola, Ohrid is a blend of cultures. As I walked ancient flagstone pathways worn smooth from centuries of use, the slap of dominoes echoed from coffee houses where old Albanian men in white caps whiled away the hours. Narrow lanes followed the contour of a rising hill, proceeding upwards to the tiny 13th century church of Sveti Jovan crouched on a precipice above the lake.

While enjoying a meal in the old town, my mind was focused on getting to Albania and completing my journey. Albania was only 12 miles away.

The next morning at 10:45 I set out from Ohrid along the ancient road that hugs the shore. I was riding on the Via Ignatia, the old Roman highway that took Roman legions from Durazzo or Durres on the Adriatic to Serbia and beyond that to Dacia or Romania. The Via Ignatia connected the western and eastern halves of the empire and was the road from Rome to Constantinople or Byzantium.

Cycling past Ohrid's airport, I arrived in Struga an hour later. This was the last Macedonian town before climbing to the mountaintop that is the Albanian frontier.

Even though I was physically still in Macedonia, in Struga I had entered the Albanian world. Coming upon a group of school children, I asked if they were Macedonian or Albanian. "Albanian!," they proclaimed. When they learned I was American, they cheered and shouted "New York" and "USA good." This deep affinity of Albanians for Americans dates from 1999 and the Kosovo war when the U.S. intervened to halt Serbia's ethnic cleansing of the Albanian majority in Kosovo. For nearly three months U.S. aircraft bombed Serbian targets—including Belgrade—eventually forcing Serbia to withdraw from Kosovo.

After this break, I began the long climb up to the border. From Struga the road ascended steeply up a strenuous 10% grade. For the first time I was compelled to zigzag as I found it impossible to go straight. I stopped every few minutes and was aware of my fast beating heart. Once I was tempted to join a shepherd who was fast asleep in a field, his staff beside him where it had fallen from his hand. At 2 PM—having traveled a mere two miles in an hour—I arrived at the border.

Atop this 1,230-meter mountain with magnificent views of Lake Ohrid and the Albanian mountains, it was very cold.

I pulled from a pannier my heaviest jacket and put it on as I waited to go through customs where I paid the $10 to enter Albania and then rode on.

# VIII.

# ALBANIA

When I planned my journey across Eastern Europe, I worried about safety only in Kaliningrad, Russia and Albania. Kaliningrad turned out to be fine. But now I was in Albania, until recently the poorest and least accessible country in Europe. During 46 years of Stalinist dictatorship that ended only in 1991 Albania's borders were sealed. People couldn't have cars. Religious practice was forbidden in the world's first officially atheist state.

My route across Albania

As I prepared for the last 100 miles of the ride, I thought about how this tiny country—the size of Vermont—had been so deeply impacted by one man, Enver Hoxha, the ultra-orthodox communist who was Albania's supreme leader for 40 years.

Hoxha was unwavering in his loyalty to the Soviet Union and Joseph Stalin, so much so that when his one-time mentor Tito defied Stalin and said Yugoslavia would pursue its own path to communism, Hoxha denounced Tito as a traitor and severed relations with Yugoslavia. Later in 1960 when Krushchev called attention to Stalin's excesses, Hoxha broke with Russia and embraced China's brand of communism. But when Mao Zedong received Richard Nixon in Beijing in 1972 an enraged Hoxha ended Albania's alliance with China. At that point Albania retreated into isolation.

A larger-size bunker, near Elbasan

Beginning in 1975 Hoxha became convinced that Albania faced imminent invasion, either from the east or from the west. Accordingly he ordered 700,000 bunkers built for defense— that's one bunker for every four Albanians, 24 bunkers in every square kilometer of territory. Of various sizes, these bizarre fortifications reveal Hoxha's thinking. He must have thought an invading army—whether NATO or Warsaw Pact—would march in formation across the land.

I contemplated all of this as I waited in the queue to enter Albania from Macedonia. At the time I was still atop the mountain and worried about my personal safety in what had been in the 1990s a violent and chaotic land.

I was now only two or three days' riding from my destination, the port of Durres on the Adriatic coast. So after a rest at the border I resumed the journey. Coming down the mountain the descent was the steepest I had experienced. The road was narrow and the switchbacks constant. As I quickly stole an upward glance, I observed what looked like a layer of cars and trucks spiraling down a totem pole.

When I reached the valley floor there was the usual crush of people and activity that is typical in Albania. It was a sharp contrast to the slower rhythms of Slavic Macedonians. Every few yards on the shoulders of the road cars were being washed or repaired. Hawkers were selling shoelaces, kitchen supplies, soft drinks, whatever. There was continual honking and vehicles pulling off. There were many construction sites and from these unfinished structures the red and black Albanian flag usually flew from the highest point. Crowded minibuses rattled past.

Albania has only three million people in a land that is 70% mountains, but it is congested and dangerous for cyclists.

That many Albanian drivers are unskilled is not surprising. How could it be otherwise? I remember that on my first visit to the capital Tirana in 1995 horse carts and bicycles outnumbered cars. I also remember traveling from Tirana to Durres and seeing the carcasses of wrecked cars. They littered the roadside, their innards stripped away by scavengers. At that time, quite literally, Albanians didn't know how to drive.

I was riding on a road that paralleled a single rail track that hugged the banks of a fast-moving river. There were several tunnels. The villages along the way were crowded and shabby. Away from traffic the air was bracing, the mountain views spectacular.

Polis, Albania and the Hotel Paradiso

By 5:30 PM I was tired and ready to stop. I had traveled 45 miles through difficult terrain and was now perhaps 20 miles east of Elbasan, a city of 80,000. After a couple of unproductive inquiries about accommodation, I resolved to stop at the first hotel I saw. It was getting dark. At the town of Librazhd, a motorist told me to be on the lookout for the Hotel Brasiliero. Riding on and looking for it, what I found instead was the Hotel Paradiso, a three-storied jumble in the middle of nowhere. There were two cars in the parking lot.

A stout young man met me at the door. He said he spoke Greek and Italian. That didn't help and I doubted the truth of his assertion as my words in Spanish didn't register. But after some moments we managed to communicate, as he knew I wanted a room. He took out a sheet of paper and wrote "€15." I nodded agreement.

The young man who called himself Don escorted me to a second floor room in the back with a balcony overlooking the river that noisily cascaded over rocks that spilled down from the mountain. On the exterior landing stood a tall wire cage that confined a small white and black songbird like a chickadee. Trying to escape the bird fluttered helplessly from one side of the cage to the other. Reaching my room and exhausted from the day's ride, I cared little that there was a crack along the full length of the mirror or that only a sliver of dirty soap lay on the washbasin, or that an empty detergent container had been left in the bathtub.

It was enough, I thought, that there was hot water, electricity, and a bed with pillow and blanket. The room's saving grace was its balcony that overlooked the rushing river and a wall of jagged rock on the far side.

After a shower I came downstairs hungry and thirsty. Don beckoned me into a cavernous dining room where I was the only patron. An older woman who might have been his mother sat behind the bar. A younger man, perhaps a brother, came from the kitchen to watch a game show that blared from a black and white TV. I ordered a Tirana beer. Don came over carrying a cutting board upon which was an uncooked steak, another kind of sliced meat, a potato and tomato. He wanted to know my preference. I chose the steak, a salad, and a potato. It was very good. My bill for the meal, beer, glass of wine, and room was €26.

I slept well, excited at the prospect of reaching Durres and completing the journey. In fact it felt like a dream about to come true. The morning arrived clear but with strong winds sweeping out of the mountains towards the sea. I loaded the bike and struggled to get in the saddle and move onto the highway. The wind was powerful. Gusts literally howled making it immediately apparent that I couldn't ride in such conditions. Pushing the bike back into the lot, I dreaded the prospect of being stranded in the bleak Hotel Paradiso for an entire day. Luckily, by mid-morning the winds had dissipated. Cautiously I conducted a test, riding slowly a quarter mile down the mountain with the wind at my back. It felt OK as I no longer feared being blown over. I returned to the Paradiso, claimed the remainder of my luggage, and bade farewell to my hosts.

* * *

The highway continued its downward slope and the wind that swept along the Shkumbin River gradually weakened to a stiff breeze. In an hour's time I reached Elbasan, the large city situated in a plain with mountains on the north and south sides. Elbasan was booming and hardly recognizable from my last visit years earlier. The vast communist-era steel mill west of town that stretches on for a quarter mile was still there but it had become a rusting hulk. Smoke curled up only from a single blast furnace. The complex had been privatized and new Turkish owners were trying to keep it going, providing jobs to a few hundred. The Chinese had built the massive "Steel of the Party" complex during Hoxha's Maoist period and it used to employ 12,000 workers.

Riding on and delighted to be on flat terrain, I glanced occasionally at the hideous bunkers that peeked out everywhere.

Near Elbasan two hikers approaching on the shoulder were obviously not Albanian. They recognized that I too was a foreigner, so we stopped to talk. They were Catholic monks from Belgium who were walking to Jerusalem as part of a pilgrimage for world peace. They had departed from St. Michelle in Normandy 11 months earlier. They said they had found Albanians hospitable and the countryside safe.

An hour later, stopping at a small cafe I came upon the classic portrait of English poet Lord Byron prominently displayed on a sidewall. The portrait is a fixture throughout Albania.

On my first visit, I had observed the Byron likeness in hotel lobbies, restaurants and public places. They are copies of an 1813 painting by Thomas Phillips. George Gordon Byron, Lord Byron, four years earlier at age of 21 had traveled for ten days in Albania, which was then part of the Ottoman Empire. Byron was smitten with the wild beauty of northern Greece and Albania and became a passionate advocate of Greek independence.

Lord Byron in Albanian garb, painted by Thomas Phillips in 1813.
Source Wikipedia (in the public domain).

By his own account, the poet became "instantly famous" upon the release of his autobiographical *Childe Harold's Pilgrimage*, a long work that was hailed as brilliant. When asked to sit for Phillips, Byron insisted on wearing the colorful turban, sash and jacket that he had acquired in Albania.

Thinking about Byron, I reflected on his travel in Albania and how different it was from mine, or from that of the austere monks trudging along and sleeping in the rough. The aristocratic Byron entered Albania from northern Greece and traversed the high mountains some 80 miles south of Elbasan. While unquestionably a pathfinder, his mode of travel was extravagant.

The diary kept by his companion J.C. Hobhouse revealed that the equestrian party included bearers carrying "four leather trunks weighing 80 pounds, three smaller trunks, three beds with bedding and two light wooden bedsteads." Hobhouse wrote, "we had heard that in Asiatic Turkey bedsteads are always service-able, preserving you from vermin, and the damp of mud floors." It was as if Byron was on safari.

Byron was fascinated by fierce Albanian tribesmen and wrote the first part of *Childe Harold* in Albania. Stanzas 52 and 53 in Canto 2 described a mysterious mountain land:

> *Morn dawns; and with it stern Albania's hills, ... Robed half in mist, bedew'd with snowy rills, Array'd in many a dun and purple streak, Arise; and as the clouds along them break, Disclose the dwelling of the mountaineer; Here roams the wolf, the eagle whets his beak, Birds, beasts of prey, and wilder men appear...*
>
> *Now Harold felt himself at length alone, and bade to Christian tongues a long adieu; Now he adventured on a shore unknown, Which all admire, but many dread to view: ... The scene was savage, but the scene was new...*

That was Byron's Albania—wild and remote:

> *Land of Albania let me bend mine eyes on thee, thou rugged nurse of savage men.*

Albanians revere Byron because he was the first famous westerner to embrace their land and their fight for liberty. Byron introduced Albania to the world.

At 1:45 that afternoon I came to Rrogozhine where the road from Macedonia that I had followed ends in a T-junction. To the right and left was Albania's north-south highway. I turned north for what would be a short ride to my destination, the Adriatic port city of Durres. There were no more mountains and a signpost indicated Durres was only 24 miles away.

Proceeding north there was heavy traffic. Luckily the shoulder was wide and the road's surface not rutted. At 3:20 PM I was in the outskirts of Durres, the fabled Durazzo of the Venetians and before that the Roman port of Dyrrachhium.

Soon I came upon the calm blue waters of the Adriatic Sea. It was a thrill and I felt a rush of accomplishment. Small waves lapped onto the shore and there were pleasant sea breezes like those I had experienced back in Latvia. I had done it, traveled all the way from the Baltic to the Adriatic!

Durres like much of Albania was utterly transformed, triumphantly modernized by enterprising Albanians since freedom arrived in 1991. As the highway morphed into the town's main thoroughfare, I passed rows of high-rise condominiums, hotels and shopping plazas. Sleepy Durres had become the Miami Beach of the Albanian world.

Exhilarated by having reached my destination, I checked into the Adriatik, the best hotel in Durres. Riding the Cannondale up the circular driveway to a manicured lawn, I felt like a prince. In the lobby the new modern Albania was on full display: polished tiled floors, elegant fixtures, immaculately attired, trilingual women behind a mahogany front desk, an Italian general manager, and on the wall—of course!—a large reproduction of Phillips' *Byron*.

I checked into a room with a balcony overlooking the sea. Thrilled with the view and my own achievement, I rushed downstairs, steered the Cannondale onto the beach, stood in the sand with the bike on my shoulder and asked an attendant to snap a photo.

Mission accomplished, Adriatic beach, Durres, Albania

I felt the full thrill of success: I had done it—2,300 miles through 15 lands from the Baltic to the Adriatic. Mission accomplished. Small boats bobbed at anchor. The sea was peaceful.

On this final full day of riding, I had traveled 51 miles. In eight days I had cycled 291 miles from the Bulgaria-Macedonia border. I had climbed the toughest mountains. Examining my notebooks, since the beginning of my journey I had been in the saddle for a cumulative 45 days.

But in fact I wasn't done. I still had to get to Tirana for the flight home. Also I needed to find a box for my bicycle.

That evening I rode into the center of Durres in search of a celebratory meal. I remembered my first visit in 1995 when Durres was a ramshackle seaport with a sad collection of peeling stucco buildings. Riding near the docks much had changed. But one thing had not. Where the road comes to a halt at a beachfront barrier the communist era statue depicting an intrepid Albanian—knee raised, rifle ready—is still there heroically resisting fascist Italy's 1939 invasion.

Near that plaza are the ruins of a Byzantine wall and a round Venetian tower. Rebuilt by the Turks in the 1500s, the tower's worn masonry steps are so steep that only the most agile visitors reach the top.

Not finding an appealing restaurant, I rode back towards the Adriatik and stopped at a pizza place with outside tables. While there a tour bus from Hungary arrived and a couple dozen people tumbled out. They collected their luggage and went into the beachfront hotel next door. For me this prosaic scene encapsulated the enormous changes that have occurred. Eastern Europe, the New Europe, is becoming not only accessible but normal. Albania, sealed off for 40 years, is now a tourist destination. Hoxha must be turning in his grave.

The next morning I loaded the bike one last time and rode to the Durres train station for the short 25-mile journey to Tirana, arguably the most dynamic and fastest changing city in Europe.

My goal was to end the trip with a night in the Austrian-owned Rogner Europa Park, where I had stayed on my previous visits. In 1995 the luxurious Rogner was the first big foreign investments in post-communist Tirana.

Pushing the bike through the Durres station I climbed onto a three-coach train pulled by a vintage Czechoslovak diesel locomotive. We departed on time and soon were keeping pace with cars and trucks on the busy highway that connects Tirana and Durres. Observing the fast and expensive cars it was hard to believe that this was where I had seen so many wrecked cars in the mid 1990s.

Soon the train crossed the intersection where one highway goes north to Tirana's airport—now named for Mother Teresa—in 1995 horses and goats grazed near the uneven, much repaired single runway. Four antique MiG fighters, canvas draped over their cockpits, were parked near the tiny terminal building. The airport now is busy and modern.

Tirana lies in a shallow bowl encircled on three sides by mountains. Since 1991 its population has exploded, more than doubling to one million. Under Hoxha people were not allowed to move to Tirana from rural areas. Today a third of Albanians live in the capital.

Our train arrived at the station, which like much of Tirana was constructed during Albania's fascist period. Modernizing Tirana became a pet project of Benito Mussolini. The dictator viewed Albania as a key element of his new Roman Empire. He instructed architects to build Tirana's central core in the shape of a fasces, the bundled sticks wrapped around an ax, the fighting symbol Mussolini borrowed from the ancient Romans.

The train station lies at the northern extremity of the boulevard that sweeps south for a mile to Mussolini's House of Fascism, now Tirana University. At the midpoint are four small Florentine-style palaces that house government ministries. They've been stylishly renovated, their green shutters handsome against the yellow stucco façade.

Alighting from the train and squeezing through the chaotic street market outside, I reached the main traffic circle where the equestrian statue of Skanderbeg, the national hero, stands at the center. He was a Catholic northerner who in the 15th century fought the invading Turks but lost. Nearby is a 19th century mosque, one of only a few remaining from the Ottoman period. In the 1930s there were at least 500 mosques in Tirana. Many were destroyed in 1944's battle for Tirana involving retreating Italians and Germans and partisans.

Riding past Tirana's modernist pyramid of polished stone, built as an art museum during the final years of communism, I arrived at the Rogner. In March 1997 the Rogner became a refuge for the many journalists and diplomats who took shelter there from the anarchy that engulfed the country. The chaos followed rioting that brought down the government. The army and police force disintegrated and for a time Albania essentially had no government.

The crisis erupted after the collapse of fraudulent investment firms that fleeced Albanians of their savings by promising—and for a time paying—exorbitant rates of interest to citizens who foolishly believed this was the way the new market economy functioned. With their "investments" doubling or tripling within weeks, Tirana was swept up in a buying frenzy with people standing in line for hours to hand over their money. In fact the investment firms—with names like Vefa, Kamberi and Gjallica—were merely paying off old deposits with new ones. They had few real assets. These were classic Ponzi schemes, just like the gigantic one in New York that later brought down the once respected Bernard Madoff.

While on assignment in Albania I had watched ordinary people willingly turn over their savings to the bogus companies. People had no idea what was really going on. When the music stopped the get-rich-quick schemes toppled one after the other, their owners fleeing for their lives. There was no regulation. The government either stood aside or was complicit in the fraud. Depositors never got their money back.

During those chaotic days the Rogner resembled Rick's café in *Casablanca*. As violence escalated, few dared venture outside. Embassies and international organizations evacuated their personnel. I recall standing on the balcony of my room scanning the sky each noon to see if the Austrian Airlines flight from Vienna was still coming in. Would the airport close, would the hotel run out of food? I remember the Rogner's maintenance chief, a rotund, usually jolly Austrian who had opened the hotel, speaking ominously of defending the property if it was stormed by rioters. In the end relief came from Italian peacekeepers dropped from military helicopters to their embassy grounds behind the Rogner tennis courts.

These memories aside, it was now several years later, and on this peaceful Saturday I was scouring the city for a bicycle box so I could be on the Monday flight to Milan and home.

At the time Tirana had only two full-service bike shops. Neither had a box and I despaired of making one from discarded cardboard as I had done in Romania.

Help came from my journalist colleague Ilirian Agolli. He remembered an Albanian American he had recently interviewed who ran United Parcel Service in Albania. Ilirian gave him a call. Nuri Shafiq was intrigued and stopped by the Rogner that same afternoon. Examining the bike he said if I disassembled it down to the frame he would have someone pick it up and pack it for transport back to D.C. The cost, he thought, would be under $200. That was a deal I couldn't refuse.

Nuri was a fascinating guy. With a degree from Harvard he had returned to Albania with McKenzie, the big consulting group, and then accepted the challenge of opening the country for UPS. Nuri was interested in my journey, particularly the different cultures I had encountered. He invited me to join friends for dinner, an invitation I quickly accepted. Together with three young diplomats the five of us spent the evening talking about identity and Albanians.

As the evening wore on Nuri voiced concern that radical Islam might take hold in Albania. "The problem," he began, "is that Albanians don't know who they are." He continued, "They have constantly faced the problem of national survival... first under the Turks, then the Italians, then Stalinist communism for 46 years. They have survived by saying yes to everyone."

Religion, Nuri feared, could become a big thing for Albanians in part because all religious practice was outlawed during communism. Historically it has been divided more or less equally between Muslim, Catholic and orthodox Christianity. He said that when he first arrived few of his employees observed Ramadan. Now, he said almost all did. He feared that of the two competing forms of Islam, the secular Turkish model was weakest while the Wahabi orthodoxy of Saudi Arabia was gaining.

A century earlier Albania's complicated identity and history were analyzed by English cultural anthropologist Edith Durham. She lived several years in the mountains of northern Albania, had great affinity for tribal Albanians, and championed their independence from the Turks. In 1909 she published a memoir entitled, *High Albania.*

> *The Albanians had, and have, no allied power to come to their aid. [In the final decades of the 19th century] they threw aside plans of independence, and again made common cause with the Turk against their old enemy the Slav."*
>
> *...They did not hate the Turk less, but they hated the Slav more. Turning Moslem in numbers and thereby gaining great influence under Turkish rule, Moslem and Christian Albanian alike supported Turk against Slav.*

Generally speaking Albanians fared well under the Turks

and many rose to prominence throughout the Ottoman Empire, including several who were military commanders. An Albanian was an early rector of Cairo University.

In our time the conflict between Albanians and Slavs has focused on Kosovo, until 2008 the southernmost province of Serbia and the cradle of its orthodox church. Albanians too have a long history in Kosovo, comprising a majority of the population for at least a century. By the time Serbia's Slobodan Milosevic attempted to drive the Albanians out they were a 90% majority. In the 1999 war the United States was the principal ally of the Kosovo Albanians and the main player behind their 2008 declaration of independence.

Returning to the Rogner for my last night in Albania, my head was spinning from the contrasting, conflicting views I had just heard. I sought distraction by taking a long walk through downtown Tirana. What an incredible place it is.

Anyone who remembers Tirana's rush hour as a whir of hundreds of bicycle tires, or the anarchy of 1997, would be amazed by the modernity, order and rising prosperity of today's city. Near the Rogner stand new high-rise office buildings called The Twin Towers, a deliberate reference to the New York City and USA so adored by Albanians who may be the most pro-American people in the world.

There is something else about Albanians. They and the Poles are the most entrepreneurial people I encountered in Eastern Europe. Albanians seem always on the move, buying and selling, starting businesses. They are seldom idle.

Much of the credit for Tirana's renaissance goes to Edi Rama, a combative artist who became the city's mayor in 2000 and in 2017 is Albania's prime minister. As mayor, Rama vanquished the city's ugliness by splashing bright colors over dozens of hideous communist-era apartment blocks. Rama sought to transform buildings into works of art and in so doing gave citizens the civic pride they never had.

When I interviewed him in the mid-2000s it was clear from his restless energy that Rama was on a quest to make Tirana livable and attractive. Beyond his obsession with coloring over the drab, Rama brought some semblance of law and order to Tirana. As mayor he bulldozed the makeshift stalls and temporary structures that had been illegally and haphazardly constructed.

In a 2012 TED talk Rama said, "when colors came out everywhere, a mood of change started transforming the spirit of the people, who started to drop less litter in the streets and started to pay taxes. Beauty was giving people a feeling of being protected."

Whatever ultimately happens in the Albanian world, people are clearly better off because of what Edi Rama accomplished as mayor of Tirana.

Monday arrived. I arose at 4 AM, paid the bill and set out for the €20 taxi journey to the airport. Winding through deserted city streets, my cab passed the Era Pizzaria where in 1999 or 2000 for the first time in my life I saw waiters take orders on hand-held devices and wirelessly transmit that data to the kitchen. This technology, effortlessly employed, quickly became commonplace in a city where ten years earlier there were more horse carts and bicycles than cars.

My journey over I was flush with the satisfaction of having finished a big undertaking. And I was so happy that I had included Albania. For better or worse this little country squeezed between Italy and Greece at the edge of the Slavic world is a fascinating place, perhaps more so than anywhere in Europe.

# EPILOGUE

Since completing the bike trip in 2005, I've stayed in touch with several friends and acquaintances I met along the way. In October 2007 I returned to the Baltic States to begin work on this book. I traveled first to Tallinn and made contact with Peep Laul who had shown me such warm hospitality at his B&B in southern Estonia near the Latvian border.

I reached Peep by phone and he suggested we meet near the Maxima supermarket not far from his home. He was shopping for fish to take home to his cat. He was friendly but depressed. Peep was 57 but looked older. "My body is giving out," he lamented. He complained that his vision had deteriorated and that worsening health meant he was now getting a full pension instead of half. He had been ordered to cut his cigarette consumption.

Peep Laul, Tallinn, 2007

Barry, Klaipeda, 2007

As to the B&B in the south, there had been problems. A legal challenge forced him to drop the name 'Anne'. "I'm hoping the treasury will take some of my land to widen the Tallinn Riga highway," he said. It was clear that the bed and breakfast business near Kabli had not succeeded.

A day later I traveled south by bus. As we approached the Latvian border I looked carefully to the right hoping to glimpse the B&B that was both a welcome refuge and splendid introduction into Estonian life. In an instant I saw it. The low brown buildings were just as they were but the sign was gone. Quickly it was all behind us as we crossed into Latvia without inspection or even slowing down. Crossing a border in the Baltics had become prosaic, an uneventful passage from one European Union country to another. It was a tangible reminder of the immense progress that had occurred.

I arrived in Klaipeda, the Lithuanian seaport where my friend Saulius had found a room near the center where I could live and work for ten days. It was super to reconnect with my biking comrade and meet some of his friends in the vibrant town with such a rich but complicated history.

The garret apartment in which I resided was reached by a steep staircase whose treads bore the imprints of two centuries of footsteps. The building had gone up in 1768. Each morning I eagerly retrieved from outside the door the wicker basket that contained a boiled egg, dark bread, butter, jams and yogurt, all neatly covered with a cloth napkin.

I worked hard in Klaipeda but departed aware that I was writing the wrong book. I had produced a chronology of a journey but there was too little attention to people, their extraordinary hospitality and assistance. I knew I had to start over.

I returned to the Baltics in October 2013 determined to reconnect with people I had met. Arriving in Tallinn I phoned Peep, but sadly, learned from his wife Anne that he had died ten days earlier.

Heikki Saller and his wife Maret were doing fine. Their son was eight, their daughter was studying information technology at Tartu University. Heikki's public relations firm was prospering. I visited his offices at a new building in a smart southern suburb. He had clients from several countries. Heikki, now 43, said starting the business 13 years earlier was the best decision he ever made. He had taken on a partner and his professional staff of four included a young man from Finland. Just as he had observed a dozen years earlier, Estonian young people with languages and optimism were winners from the transition.

Heikki's conference room, 2013

I had exchanged emails with Rein Reinok, the entrepreneur in Marjamaa who had opened his home to me on the critical first day of my ride. Rein said he would be happy to see me. I phoned from Tallinn and he agreed to meet my bus in Marjamaa the next afternoon.

Rein was now 53 and had lost some of the entrepreneurial zeal so apparent a decade earlier. He had split with his Finnish partner and the solar panel business moved to Tallinn. He now worked for another company and traveled often to Finland.

Rein Reinok, Marjamaa, 2013

"It's a difficult time now in Estonia," he said, "because every-thing costs too much and it's hard to get credit." He said he often felt a prisoner of his duplex home that is paid for, because he can't find renters for the second flat. He would be willing to sell, he said, but there were no buyers. Over a home-cooked meal with his wife and two teenage sons, Rein said he likes Marjamaa too much to leave even though he had considered moving to Tallinn where his wife teaches at the technical uni-versity. "Marjamaa," he said, "is too far from Parnu and too far from Tallinn to attract new residents or business."

Later that day I again boarded the regional bus for the short journey to the coastal resort of Parnu. I was met by Enno Kuusmets, with whom I had exchanged Christmas cards. Enno was now 77 and in failing health. He had moved from his cottage in the woods to Parnu two years ago. As we rode the city bus to his apartment at the edge of town Enno told me his father had been forced into the German army in World War II. Because of that when the Russians returned in 1945, his father was sent to Siberia for ten years. His health ruined, he died two years after returning home.

Enno said when he was 19 he had hoped to study at Tartu University, but the family didn't have the bus fare for the 50-mile journey to where he would take the entrance exam. Instead Enno spent three years in the Red Army.

Enno Kuusmets, Parnu, 2013

Enno said his monthly pension was €306. Of that, he told me, €30 went for rent, €30 in tax, €30 for gas and electricity, €30 for cable TV. The remainder, €186, he said, had to cover food and everything else. Enno's apartment was in an austere, two-story communist-era building two miles from town.

As we sat in his living room having tea and cookies, I remembered that Enno had become fluent in English from home study and watching Hollywood movies on TV. Like millions of others he had endured a hard life with few of the choices we in the west take for granted. Thanking Enno for his hospitality, I took the bus back into Parnu and the next day traveled to Riga and then Klaipeda.

Saulius Rozinskas, Klaipeda, 2013

In my favorite Lithuanian town I again met Saulius Rozinskas, whose bicycle touring business was thriving as more and more cyclists were coming to the Baltics. He had recently led a group of cyclists through the Republic of Georgia. He has 200 bikes available for rent. He had just returned from a vacation cruise in the Mediterranean with his wife and two children.

My next destination was Kaliningrad. I again made the short ferry crossing to the Curonian Spit and boarded the daily bus for Zelenogradsk. I asked the driver, who didn't speak English, to drop me at the bird-tracking station at Rybachy where I was expected. In fact the driver forgot and neither he nor I noticed that we had sped past Rybachy. When we arrived in Zelenogradsk he was apologetic. Luckily there were waiting cabs at the bus station and a driver who spoke English offered to take me back for €15. Off we went.

Amazingly, as we approached Rybachy the car ahead stopped to observe several large boars gathered at the side of the road. We too stopped and admired these strange creatures that had so terrified me when I traversed by bike this long, hauntingly beautiful finger of sand and forest.

Wild boars near Rybachy

Andrey Mukhin at Rybachy Biological Station

I was met at the biological station by Andrey Mukhin, a young ornithologist who is part of the team tracking birds at the facility founded by Johannes Thienemann in 1901. I had communicated with Mukhin by email explaining that I had met one of his colleagues when I came through on a bike in 2003. He invited me to visit.

The Russian scientists at Rybachy toil in primitive conditions, continuing work that has gone on with a few notable interruptions for over a century. I joined the team of six for lunch and then visited their nets along the Baltic shore where birds are caught and banded before being released. I learned from Andrey that in World War II the facility was taken over by the Luftwaffe and glider pilots trained here. It wasn't until the 1950s that the Russians reestablished the biological station.

In the afternoon Mikhail, one of Mukhin's colleagues, took me into the woods to the German cemetery that was desecrated after the Soviets arrived in 1945. The Russian scientists had recently placed a handsome granite marker over Thienemann's grave. The famous German had died here in 1938, months short of his 75th birthday. I was visiting the grave on the 150th anniversary of Thienemann's birth.

After snacks in Rybachy's lone café, the two scientists put me on the bus to Zelenogradsk where I arrived 30 minutes later. The resort town was dramatically improved with several high-rise condos and a downtown that sparkled. It had become a vacation destination for people from St. Petersburg and Moscow.

The next day I went on to Kaliningrad city where I had arranged to meet Rosa Sverdlina and her daughter Galina. Misha, the World War II veteran, had passed away. Arriving by cab I was again greeted as a long-lost friend by the two women who had prepared a wonderful lunch in their second-floor walkup near the city center. Regrettably, unlike my emotional visit in 2003, there was no one to translate. Thus necessarily our time together lacked the poignancy of that earlier meeting.

Rosa Sverdlina and daughter Galina, Kaliningrad, 2013

By May 2014 the book I wanted, emphasizing people as well as cycling, was coming together. But to finish I needed to reconnect with friends in the Balkans to see how they were doing. Was this poorest part of New Europe making at least some gains and thus not falling too far behind faster-growing Central Europe and the Baltics?

I returned to Sofia and found the Bulgarian capital little changed. Old Hungarian Ikarus buses still rolled through the shabby downtown. People complained that European Union membership in 2007 hadn't improved their lives. Mikhail, a young man who sold me a SIM card for my phone, complained that Bulgaria got nothing from the EU. "We're at the periphery of Europe," he said, "and treated as third world."

The next day I traveled north in a rented car following in reverse the route I cycled nine years earlier. It took nearly five hours to reach still impoverished Vidin, the river town adjacent to the new EU-financed bridge over the Danube. Heavy spring rains had left the rutted streets of Vidin nearly impassable, which appeared in even worse condition than in 2005.

The northwest region where Vidin is situated is the poorest part of Bulgaria, which in turn is the poorest EU country. Average annual wages in Bulgaria are just over €4,000.

I hurried on to Romania, surprised that mine was the only vehicle on the magnificent new road and rail bridge, a gift of the European Union. My first impression was that Romania was doing somewhat better than Bulgaria. The highway between Calafat and Turnu Severin had been resurfaced. The water wells that I had observed in villages were still there but not being used, a clear indication that residential water lines had been built.

After spending the night in Turnu Severin, I drove on to Doina's riverboat restaurant, eager to reconnect with the Tufis family, my friends from 1999 and my window into the Iron Gate region. Pulling into the empty parking lot, the first person I saw was Jimmy, who as a boy on my first visit proudly showed me his swans and ducks.

Doina and family, 2014

We were delighted to see each other. Jimmy, now 29, cradled his two-year-old daughter in his arms as he explained he had stayed only one year in Australia. Things hadn't gone well there, he said, so he returned to Romania. Without work and drawing €100 per month in unemployment, Jimmy and his family live not far from the boat restaurant in Baile Herculane.

Not surprisingly I found Doina in the galley, perspiring from the heat from large pots on the stove. Silviu arrived, kissed me on both cheeks and asked that I stay for lunch. Later when we were seated and relaxed, Doina told me her story. It was clear that times were tough. Another restaurant had opened nearby and the need for business meant that she no longer shooed away the truckers who did business with prostitutes in the parking lot. "There is so much corruption," she said. "Romania needs a king," she continued, "maybe then people would have respect and change their corrupt ways."

Doina complained about the weak economy. "When people come to the restaurant they often share one drink. They have no money and no jobs," she said. Things are bad, she emphasized, despite some appearances to the contrary. The quality of education, she said, was atrocious and better during communism. "Now," she continued, "you can simply buy a diploma or get a good grade by giving €20 to the teacher. During communism," she went on, "we lived in a cage and now things are wide open with no rules. You have money only if you work for the government." It was disheartening to hear all this and to see Doina under such stress.

Nikolaus Luncan in Bakova's church, 2014

I then drove north through the Cerna Valley to Lugoj and west to Bakova to see Nikolaus Luncan, the sturdy German-speaking Romanian who met me outside the village church in 2004. I found Nikki (Nikolaus), now 59, at his home diagonally across the street from the church whose steeple was a landmark as I cycled east from Timisoara.

Nikki told me that there were now 20 or so Germans in Bakova, most of them retirees who have recently returned home from Germany. We visited the church that had been renovated with donations sent from German churches. Nikki then showed me the carpentry workshop behind his house. It was filled with an impressive array of tools including handcrafted chisels and clamps. Wood shavings covered the floor. Nikki complained that there wasn't enough demand for his work. Before I departed Nikolaus told me his financial situation, which seemed OK. He said his pension was the equivalent of €200 per month. In addition his wife sent money from Austria. Their daughter lives and works in Bavaria.

Adrian Maran, Timisoara, 2014

My final stop was Timisoara, where my friend Adrian Maran was the general manager of a downtown hotel. Adi had not had an easy time as things didn't work out with his Canadian girlfriend and there were also problems with the new love of his life, a Romanian woman from the Black Sea coast.

Always a keen observer of Romanian politics, Adi assured me that not much had changed since his country became a member of the European Union. Corruption, he emphasized, remained a very large problem. Despite challenges, Adi was doing well. Timisoara appeared prosperous.

As I drove back to Sofia over the roads I had traveled on my bicycle odyssey, I was sad that Romania and Bulgaria had registered so little progress over the past decade. On both sides of the Danube I saw as many horse carts as in 2004 and 2005. Aside from infrastructure projects like the Danube bridge and resurfaced roadways, I saw few improvements in peoples' lives. My friends—usually upbeat—were pessimistic, complaining about high prices and the exodus of young people to Western Europe.

In September 2015 I returned to Macedonia to see friends and survey the mountains I had crossed on a bike. I wanted to see if the mountains were as formidable as they seemed ten years earlier.

Isak, Skopje, 2015

Isak Ramadani, my longtime friend in Skopje, was doing well, still reporting on Macedonian affairs. His family was well and their living and work situations were solid. Ethnic Albanians like Isak continually held ministerial posts in the Macedonian government and despite recurrent friction the two groups were getting along relatively well. Greece, no matter if the government in Athens was conservative or liberal, remained hostile to Macedonia, demanding that its name be changed. Greece was still blocking Macedonia's membership in NATO and the European Union.

From Skopje I traveled 3½ hours by bus to Bitola, the southern city where in Turkish times Kemal Ataturk attended military school. The bus traversed roads I cycled in 2005. We crossed Pletvar Pass and I saw again the 998-meter marker for the summit that I had struggled to reach. To my surprise Pletvar seemed even more formidable than I remembered.

Trifun presenting me with a bottle of Macedonian wine, Bitola, 2015

Bitola remains as charming as it was although its agricultural hinterland was economically depressed. I found the De Niro Hotel where I stayed, but it had closed a year earlier. Trifun, the waiter and my host in 2005, now owned a downtown lighting store. We met for coffee and caught each other up on what had gone on in our lives. Trifun hadn't changed. He was as cynical and angry about Macedonian politics as when we first met. He raged on about the corruption in Skopje and was particularly harsh about the weak economy, which he said had caused a huge outflow of talented young people from Bitola. "They go anywhere they can," he said, "to find work, to Western Europe, America and even Australia."

\* \* \*

So, we've reached the end. What conclusions can be drawn? I offer three.

*Number one*, freedom triumphed for 110 million people behind the Iron Curtain when communism collapsed and the Soviet Union withdrew from Eastern Europe.

Fear and oppression were banished, the human spirit set free. Dreams of independence and integration with a free and democratic Europe were fulfilled.

*Number two*, the transformation from state control to democracy and free markets has been a success, far more so than was predicted in 1990.

In the dozen or so countries that I came to know, the essential institutions of a free society—private property, rule of law, independent judiciary, freedom of speech, free elections, independent media—have taken hold, albeit with variations country to country.

*Number three*, progress has been uneven with the fastest reformers—the Central Europeans and Baltics doing best, the Balkans lagging. A negative throughout the region is income inequality and the elderly are often struggling. But for most people in New Europe living standards have been steadily improving.

David Lipton, the American deputy director of the International Monetary Fund who was active in the Polish reforms, credits the success of transformation to "great people, smart strategies, and external support." I agree. From the perspective of 25 years ago, even modest success was not assured.

It was, I think, an extraordinary act of statesmanship that the European Union in 2004 extended membership to seven of the formerly communist lands through which I traveled. This, plus membership in the North Atlantic Treaty Organization, anchored the Baltics, Poland, the Czech Republic, Slovakia, and Hungary in the west. Romania and Bulgaria joined the EU in 2007. Some of the countries I crossed—Serbia, Macedonia, Albania—are still knocking on the door, and Kaliningrad as part of Russia is a special case. Make no mistake, the European dream is still alive.

As to riding a bicycle in New Europe, do it. These are welcoming, diverse countries with rich traditions from which much can be learned. New Europe in 2017, particularly beyond the capital cities, remains *terra incognita* for most travelers.

They are fun places and they're waiting for you.

BARRY D. WOOD is a writer and broadcaster in Washington, DC. He is the international economics correspondent for *RTHK* radio in Hong Kong, and contributes to *marketwatch.com*, *USA Today*, and *biznews.com* in South Africa. His first overseas travel was a five-month stint in 1963 as a deck boy on the Swedish freighter *Parrakoola* from San Francisco to Australia. Later he worked on Norwegian and Dutch passenger liners. For over two decades Barry was the chief economics correspondent at *Voice of America*, during which time he reported from more than 60 countries. He comes from Grand Rapids, Michigan and has B.A. and M.A. degrees in economics from Western Michigan University, with short-term study at Oxford and in Yugoslavia. His website is www.econbarry.com.

95762113R00114

Made in the USA
Lexington, KY
13 August 2018